THE HUMAN WORK OF ART

*A Theological Appraisal of Creativity
and the Death of the Artist*

The Human Work of Art

A Theological Appraisal of Creativity and the Death of the Artist

by

DAVOR DŽALTO

ST VLADIMIR'S SEMINARY PRESS

YONKERS, NEW YORK

2014

Library of Congress Cataloging-in-Publication Data

Džalto, Davor, 1980–
    The human work of art : a theological appraisal of creativity and the death of
the artist / by Davor Džalto.
        pages cm
    Includes bibliographical references.
    ISBN 978–0–88141–501–8 (paper) — ISBN 978–0–88141–502–5 (electronic)
    1. Creative ability—religious aspects—Orthodox Eastern Church.
2. Art and religion.   3. Creation.   4. Theological anthropology.   5. Orthodox
Eastern Church—Doctrines.   6. Zizioulas, Jean, 1941–.   I. Title.
    BX342.9.M35D38 2014
    261.5'7—dc23

                                                2014024512

COPYRIGHT © 2014 BY
Davor Džalto

ST VLADIMIR'S SEMINARY PRESS
575 Scarsdale Road, Yonkers, NY 10707
1-800-204-2665
www.svspress.com

ISBN 978–088141–501–8

PRINTED IN THE UNITED STATES OF AMERICA

Contents

Acknowledgments

I am deeply grateful to the many individuals and institutions who helped me through the process of research and writing this book. Without them, this project would have never been completed.

I owe a huge debt of gratitude to his Excellency Archbishop Stanislav Hočevar for his continuous support of my work.

This book is based on my post-doctoral project that was conducted at the Faculty of Catholic Theology of the University of Münster. The research and my stay in Münster would not have been possible without the support of the Katholischer Akademischer Ausländer Dienst (KAAD), and the Faculty of Catholic Theology. I will always be thankful to both for this memorable experience.

I am also deeply grateful to Prof. Thomas Bremer and Prof. Reinhard Hoeps for their invaluable help during my stay in Münster. I will never be able to repay them for their advices, suggestions, and their friendship.

I must also express my gratitude to the late Fr. Radovan Bigović, a dear friend and collaborator in many initiatives. I will continue to treasure the memory of his friendship and support while regretting that he passed away without having seen this project completed.

This book would never have appeared, at least not in this form, without the kind help of two excellent scholars and dear friends: Prof. Michelle Facos and Prof. Aristotle Papanikolaou. Their comments and suggestions significantly improved the manuscript. My gratitude extends to Professor and Father John Behr as well, not only for his excellent remarks and suggestions, but also for helping me formulate the title of this book.

At the beginning of my research, I benefited from substantial help from Prof. Anna Williams. She invested a lot of time providing comments and sharing her thoughts on a variety of subjects.

My gratitude also extends to his Eminence John Zizioulas, whose ideas inspired much of my work. I am grateful for his interest in this topic, and for the time we spent discussing some of the issues related to this work.

I would also like to take this opportunity to thank numerous friends and colleagues in the United States, Serbia, Germany, and elsewhere, who were irreplaceable partners for countless discussions that helped me sharpen my ideas and engender new ones.

Although this may be an unusually long acknowledgment section, given the size of the book itself, I do have one important final "thank you." It always seems somewhat pathetic when authors use one of the first pages in their book to carry on about their family members. However, keeping in mind that academic practices are very conservative in their nature, I thought that it would be a smart idea not to break with this important tradition. Therefore I would like to take a moment to sincerely thank my wife Bojana for the patience and understanding (not without occasional complaints) she has had for my creative work, for the time and passion necessary to carry it out.

D. Dž.

Illustrations

Abbreviations

AB – *The Anchor Bible*
ABD – *The Anchor Bible Dictionary*
DB – *Dictionary of the Bible*
DTIB – *Dictionary for Theological Interpretation of the Bible*
EDR – *Encyclopedic Dictionary of Religion*
EP – *Enzyklopädie Philosophie*
HWP – *Historisches Wörterbuch der Philosophie*
IB – *The Interpreter's Bible*
IDB – *The Interpreters Dictionary of the Bible*
LTK – *Lexikon für Theologie und Kirche*
NDT – *The New Dictionary of Theology*
NHTG – *Neues Handbuch theologischer Grundbegriffe*
ODJR – *The Oxford Dictionary of the Jewish Religion*
PG – *Patrologia Graeca*
PGL – *A Patristic Greek Lexicon*

Introduction

I Background and Objectives of the Study

"Creation" and "creativity" are frequently used concepts in our culture today. Since the beginning of the modern age, "creativity" has occupied quite an important place in the history of Western ideas. To speak of creativity as a significant anthropological concept, particularly in the field of "fine arts" (*beaux arts*), is the legacy of the Enlightenment period.[1] Apart from the context of the art world, in which creativity has dominantly been used over the last two hundred years, this concept characterizes nowadays almost all possible varieties of the human endeavor. We very often hear not only of creative individuals (e.g., artists) or creative arts, but also creative science, creative management, creative writing, creative cooking and so forth.

The concepts of creation and creativity[2] come to European ("western") civilization from the Judeo-Christian tradition and the biblical narratives. It is here, in the very first line of the Old Testament, where we find the idea of *creation*. We are informed that God *created* "the

---

[1] Pierre Macherey even states that "The proposition that the writer or artist is a creator belongs to a humanist ideology." See Macherey, 1978: 66.

[2] "Creation" and "creativity" have sometimes been understood as different concepts, if not even opposite in their meaning. Rob Pope, for instance (in respect to George Steiner's argument on creation), understands the concept of "creativity" as "a broadly human and potentially more—than or other—than human process" while "creation" refers to "a narrowly artistic and ultimately divinely legitimated process" (Pope, 2005: 32). I do not intend to make such distinctions. On the contrary, I understand human "creativity" here as a capacity which enables "creation" as a particular *act* and *event*.

heaven and the earth" (Gen 1.1). Although the creative acts of God have
been carefully studied in the history of Christian theology, the idea that
human beings can be creative and thus create attracted notably little
attention among theologians. Creation *ex nihilo* has been considered
an exclusive capacity of God to such an extent that the title "Creator"
became almost another name for God in his relation to the world, similar to other titles of God such as "Lord" and "Almighty." On the other
hand, the human being is *only* a creature (although quite distinguished
among other creatures in many respects) and as a creature "cannot itself
create."[3] However, it has usually been held that human beings can shape

---

[3]Cf. Pope: "The orthodox Christian view, propounded by St Augustine and
reinforced by St Thomas Aquinas, was that 'the creature cannot itself create' (crea-
tura non potest creare). This was based upon the biblical account in which Adam
and Eve have the power of 'naming' the other creatures but not of actually creating them (Genesis 2.19)." (Pope, 2005: 45) In addition, it can be added that the
very Hebrew verb "to create" (*bara*) is reserved for God's creative acts exclusively,
throughout the Old Testament narrative (cf. Jenson, 2004: 18–20). In his further
analysis of the concept of "creation" Pope shows that "creation" in the medieval
texts always refers to God's act of creation (see Pope, 2005: 37). Later on, the concept
began to slowly be used in the context of human activities, but it took quite a long
time until it was liberated from its divine connotations: "Only gradually and fitfully
did a specifically human sense of agency creep into the meaning of 'create'. But even
then human powers of creation tended to be tinged—or tainted—with a divine
aura. This is the point of the jibe in Shakespeare's *The Comedy of Errors* (III.2.39;
c. 1594): 'Are you a God? Would you create me new?' In fact, throughout the six-
teenth and seventeenth centuries, purely human 'creation' was commonly viewed
with suspicion, as something delusive and potentially harmful." (Pope, 2005: 38)
Following Pope, it is the eighteenth century when this concept began to signify
"human creation" and this tendency, one should note, corresponds with the birth
of the modern "subject" or "individual," without any need for theological foundations ("By the eighteenth century, however, there was a much more positive link
being forged between the power of the human 'Mind' and the capacity to 'create'
productive mental images [i.e., Imagination]. Thus Mallet [. . .] can speak in the
same breath of 'the Muse, Creative Power, Imagination.' And by the close of the
eighteenth century there is a growing sense that when humans 'create' this entails
the fashioning of something new or novel in contradistinction to the 'imitation'

many different forms out of rough (pre-given) matter, despite the fact that they are unable to create in the absolute meaning of the word (*ex nihilo*). By the means of *artistic skills*, these forms can be made *beautiful*, which resembles in some respects the variety of God's creative acts and the beauty of his works. This was generally the basis upon which virtually all of the comparisons between God and the artist in the patristic literature were constructed.

However, if the question of human creative capacities is reduced to the question of the production of material things that are both useful and beautiful, it becomes clear that human creativity is not considered to be a concept that has immediate ontological significance. It is, then, primarily understood as a *techno-logical* and *aesthetic* concept, as a capacity to transform nature in order to make it useful for humans' own ends and to make human surroundings *beautiful*.[4] The focus is on the human calling to cultivate the world and shape beautiful, harmonious forms, witnessing to the divine origin of the world and, possibly, to the coming Kingdom of God and its inexpressible beauty.

In the Orthodox Christian tradition the question of human creativity and its significance for broader theological interests was most prominently raised by Nikolai Berdyaev (1874–1948). This religious philosopher was probably the first one who pointed to the very serious ontological consequences of human creative capacities. He has also directly related freedom, as a mode of existence, to creativity,

---

of something old. The distinction between Imitation that is derivative ['a mere copy'] and Imagination that is creative and 'original' is central to Edward Young's *Conjectures on Original Composition . . .*." Pope, 2005: 38).

[4]This understanding of human "creation," as giving a new form to the material which is already there, to make it useful and "beautiful," is rooted into the ancient understanding of "art" as *techne* (τέχνη). *Techne* implies both *knowledge* and *skill* necessary to produce something (cf. Liddell, Scott, 1996: 1785). However, the idea that human being (as well as gods) can authentically create, which means to bring into being something that has never existed before, seems to be absent from the ancient Greek cosmology and ontology.

examining this relation not through the prism of aesthetics but through Christian ontology, soteriology, and eschatology. However, his thought can hardly be regarded as an Orthodox theological approach in the strict meaning of the word. Despite the fact that most of his philosophy was inspired by the Orthodox and Christian tradition, many topics of Berdyaev's philosophy seem to challenge, or to be incompatible with the dominant theological discourses in Orthodox theology.[5]

The question of human creation/creativity and art, together with the important repercussions it might have on the meaning of human existence and Christian anthropology in general, was raised again within contemporary Orthodox theological discourse in the work of John Zizioulas. He addresses this question from a strictly theological perspective and tries to shed light on the basic capacities of the human being. His analysis, to which I will refer later, provides important insights into creativity as a basic human category. However, since the purpose of his interest in human creative capacities and art was to develop an anthropological and soteriological argument, he never made it the central issue of his research, nor did he develop any Orthodox theology of the arts in his corpus.

Apart from the question of a theology of human creativity as such, a theological articulation of modern and contemporary visual arts as phenomena has attracted notably little attention among theologians. This is unfortunate because I believe such a theological articulation would yield important content for reflection on the Christian experience of the world. Any analysis of the issues that modern and contemporary art provoke in relation to basic theological questions has been a

---

[5]Some of the most remarkable ideas that, in the eyes of many, set Berdyaev's thought apart from the established dogmas are his ideas of "Ungrund," "third revelation in Spirit" as well as the idea of change within the being of God. For general insight into relations between Berdyaev and the early Fathers see Begzos, 1993.

rarity in Orthodox theological discourse.[6] I think that there are several reasons for this.

The first reason has to do with the strong presence of one type of visual representation that has dominated the Orthodox Christian tradition—the icon. Since icons are by definition figurative and mimetic representations, and deeply rooted in Orthodox theology, it became quite difficult to accept and theologically contemplate modern art in form of abstract paintings, for instance, not to mention other expanded media such as ready-mades, land-art, or performances. It should also be taken into account that the formal qualities as well as contents of modern and contemporary art might have seemed to many theologians very distant from the Christian world-view, if not trivial and unworthy of serious attention.

I believe that the second reason for the lack of theological appreciation of modern and contemporary western art has to do with the state of Orthodox theology in the twentieth century. While going through a renaissance, after a long period of stagnation and "imprisonment," Orthodox theology found itself preoccupied with more urgent questions that needed to be clarified (e.g., ecclesiological, liturgical, eschatological, and anthropological matters) before the question of modern art could be seriously addressed.

There is probably another, more general reason for the split between theology and modern/contemporary art, one that goes beyond the boundaries of Orthodox theology. It is the very character of the dominant tendencies within modern art, manifested in the quest for the *autonomy* of art. In other words, art of the twentieth century not only ceases to be representational (figurative) in many of its manifestations,

[6]However, some steps in the form of theological reflections upon particular aesthetical phenomena have been made in respect to early modern art (see Berdyaev, 1918; Berdyaev, 1996-a, Vol. II; Skliris, 2005). The most important contribution to the reflections on art and Orthodox theology (including some manifestations of modern art) were given by Paul Evdokimov (see Evdokimov, 2001; Evdokimov, 2004) and Paul Florensky (see Florensky, 1915; Florensky, 2002).

it also tries to define itself in a tautological manner, refusing any other relation except its own purposes, contents, and means.

It is true, however, that apart from these tendencies, we also find opposite approaches in twentieth-century art where it becomes quite intensely socially involved. Many modern artists were not afraid to use their art to respond to the social and political challenges of the day. But even this opening of art toward the world has not helped in bridging the gap between modern art and Christianity. Many of these socially and politically involved individuals and movements were very critical toward ideologies, religion, and various social institutions. Sometimes they were openly and consciously atheistic, anti-religious, and even blasphemous.[7] All of this might have contributed to the situation in which theology and Christianity in general parted ways with modern and contemporary art.[8]

Finally, it seems that there is also a problem of the method theologians have employed in their reflections on art. Theological reflections on art have traditionally suffered from looking upon art as a maidservant whose purpose is to illustrate theological views and Christian narratives, or to express "beauty" (whatever we take it to be) as a topic that one can explore within the realm of theological aesthetics. This might have caused difficulties in comprehending art that does not serve those purposes and that cannot be treated simply as an aesthetic object.

[7]To show that, it is enough to recall many of the Dadaist, Futurist and Constructivist interventions, or late twentieth-century works such as "Crucified Frog" by Martin Kippenberger or "Piss Christ" by Andres Serrano. However, this does not mean that Christian motifs and explicit references to religious narratives were never portrayed in an affirmative or, at least neutral, light in twentieth-century art. Christian iconography has been an important point of reference to some of the most influential artists within particular movements and tendencies of modern and contemporary art, from Georges Rouault to Joseph Beuys and Marina Abramović.

[8]James Elkins articulates the problem of separation and even mutual hostility between religion and contemporary art in his work *On the Strange Place of Religion in Contemporary Art*. See Elkins, 2004.

Contrary to these approaches, my intention in this study is two-fold:

1. To explain human creative capacities and explore their significance for Orthodox Christian anthropology

2. To analyze particular modern and contemporary artworks and artistic practices in order to develop a theological argument in respect to human creative capacities.

None of the examples of artworks and art practices that will be analyzed here exploit Christian motifs or iconography, nor can they be considered "Christian" or "religious" in any formal sense.

II Structure

The study is divided into four chapters. It is my hope that the following structure will help to present in an approachable manner the whole variety of issues that appear in the text.

Having explained the main objectives of the study and its place in relation to the previous research in this field, my intention in chapter one is to present the theses that human creation can and should be considered an authentic creation (*ex nihilo*) and that human creativity represents a vital aspect of the image of God in the human being. In order to explain why it is essential to take human creative capacities into account when building a successful Orthodox Christian anthropology, I give a brief outline of God's creative acts and how they impact the understanding of his being, in relation to the world and human beings. I develop this analysis based on twentieth-century Orthodox personalism; I make explicit references to Vladimir Lossky and John Zizioulas, but the general style of the argument also follows Nikolai Berdyaev's personalism. Based on this, I draw a parallel between the capacities of creation and freedom, both in the case of God and in the case of human beings. In the second part of this chapter I present John Zizioulas' argument on human creative capacities, which I intend to examine critically in my later analysis. I also give a brief account on the context of Zizioulas' argument on creativity within his theology of personhood. After defining the problem, I present a couple of central questions in respect to human creative capacities that I intend to explore in the subsequent chapters.

The second chapter of the study represents the central part in which I develop my argument and present an analysis of particular examples of twentieth-century art—"ready-mades" by Marcel Duchamp, *Le Vide* by Yves Klein and "absence works" by Richard Long, Andy Warhol, and Donald Rodney. The goal in this chapter is to explain the ontological significance of creativity based on an analysis of these examples. I also address the creative act as a solution to the problem of necessity that human beings face in their fallen state (i.e., the necessity of the pre-given world and individuality). Finally, in this context I discuss the issue of creativity and artistic practice in respect to time and Christian eschatology.

In the third chapter I synthesize the previously explained arguments and insights. Based on the analysis of particular modern and contemporary art phenomena, I explain the potential theological significance of these developments in twentieth-century art. I also give an outline of the possible ways in which thinking on the aesthetics of a creative act might be further developed.

Titles of publications as well as quotations that are originally written in languages other than English and German (e.g., in Serbian, Greek, or Russian) are translated by the author for the purposes of this text. Titles of these publications appear in the body of the text only in their English translation and are listed in the bibliography first in English and then in the original version, in parentheses. Authors whose names originally appear in other alphabets (e.g., Greek or Cyrillic letters) are given in the body of the text and in bibliography in the Latin transcription.

CHAPTER 1

Creation and Artistic Practice

1.1 Artistic Production and Human Creative Capacities

Drawing parallels between the work of the artist and God's creative acts goes back to early Christian religious-philosophical reflections on art. As Victor V. Bychkov explains, comparisons between God and the artist were common to the "whole spiritual atmosphere of the late antiquity."[1] Although Christianity has redefined many aspects of the ancient worldview (especially in respect to some of the basic ontological, cosmological and anthropological concerns[2]), it seems that Christian

---

[1]Bychkov, 2010: 228. In his study *Aesthetics of the Church Fathers* the author offers a very precise analysis of the relations between human creative/artistic works and their divine prototype. Bychkov shows that in the history of Christian thought one can find not only the idea that the artistic (imperfect) endeavor resembles in some respects the divine (perfect) creation but also the other way around, that the very creative acts of God are understood as being basically similar to the acts of the artist (see Bychkov, 2010: 227–229). This idea made it possible to think of God as "artifex" who "becomes similar, in many respects, to the 'earthly' artist." Bychkov, 2010: 515.

[2]I refer here somewhat simplistically to the "ancient" worldview versus the "Christian" one, in spite of all complexity and variety of Greek and Roman thought (which makes it difficult to speak of only one Greek and Roman "ontology" for example), and in spite of the fact that Christian writers took over the whole conceptual apparatus of the Greeks and Romans. However, I believe that there is enough space for such generalization, at least for the purposes of this study, given the presence of certain metaphysical premises in the majority of the ancient philosophical and mythical narratives that are very remote from ontological premises that char-

---

understanding of art and artists has not followed other conceptual changes. Art and artists (at this time primarily painters and sculptors) were perceived basically in the same manner, as craftsmen who could shape useful and beautiful things by utilizing matter. However, drawing a direct parallel between God and his creative works on the one side and the artist and his *techne*-based work on the other, although logical within ancient cosmology, is highly problematic in the Christian context. There are a couple of reasons for this.

First of all, making comparisons between God and the artist entails the danger that God's creative acts might also be understood as basically shaping the already existing matter or making *order* and *beauty* out of *chaos*, which is opposite to the Christian doctrine of *creatio ex nihilo*. Although highly problematic from a Christian point of view, this is precisely what occurs in the writings of some early Christian authors who produced an amalgam of the ancient cosmology and the Christian understanding of *creatio ex nihilo*.[3]

Second, reducing the question of human creativity to the question of the skilled work of the artist (e.g., painting or sculpture), is problematic from the perspective of Christian anthropology as well. In Christian understanding the human being is the "image of God." Since the Christian God is the *Creator*, to reduce human creative capacities to the labor of the Greek *technites* is to obscure a very important aspect of this "image." In other words, it becomes unclear what differentiates

acterize the Judeo-Christian thought. For more on the relations between ancient Greek culture and Christianity see Zizioulas, 2008.

[3] Here Bychkov points primarily to Justin and Athenagoras, who both explicitly call God *technites*. However, referring to God's creation as "artistic" or to God as "artist" can also be found in the works of Irenaeus of Lyons and Minucius Felix (Bychkov, 2010:230–234). One reason for this inconsistency Bychkov sees in the intention of the Christian apologists to defend matter and the material reality from the "spiritualists" and dualists. A second reason can be found in their attempt to prove the existence of God as the creator of everything and to defend the reality of his being and presence (see Bychkov, 2010: 229).

the human being as the "image" of the Christian God from the human being as the "image" of the Greek Demiurge, where human creative capacities are concerned. Do we consider human creative capacities an essential aspect of the image of God at all?

To answer these questions it is necessary to clarify what the properties of this "image" are from an Orthodox Christian perspective, and what the relation is between them and their divine prototype.

1.1.1 THE PROTOTYPE

For Orthodox Christians God is not only the *Almighty*, he is foremost an absolutely *free* Being. God is free from all necessities, including the necessity of his own being (nature or essence). This freedom can be called ontological—meaning that a being does not face the necessity of its existence, which consequently means that its very existence is an exercise of freedom. God is ontologically free because His existence is not grounded upon a cause external to him, nor is there any inner necessity (that of nature, for instance) he must obey. There is no reason for God's existence except God's free will to exist. God exercises his free existence in a specific manner. He exists as a *communion* of three Divine Persons. The Father, the Son, and the Holy Spirit are not necessary manifestations of the nature of God. In other words, the nature (essence) of God does not ontologically precede his personhood, but the other way around, his personhood constitutes his being. This further implies that God's existence is identical not only to his freedom but also to his love. The ontological freedom of God is manifested as a communion with other persons—*a communion of love*.[4] Love should not be understood here as a sentiment or psychological property of certain individual beings; it rather represents an *ecstatic* overcoming

---

[4]Cf. Zizioulas: "it thus becomes evident that the only exercise of freedom in an ontological manner is love. Love is identified with ontological freedom." Zizioulas, 1985: 46.

of individual isolation in order to find one's true identity and life in the communion with others.

The consequence of this is that communion (being formed upon the *ekstasis*[5] of personal beings) and freedom appear as two essential capacities that constitute a mode of existence often called "person-hood." These two capacities are so closely linked that the existence of one almost necessarily implies the existence of the other.

The ontological freedom of God, as absence of any necessity which limits His existence, manifests itself not only in respect to the being of God but also in his relation to the world. In contrast to the ancient Greek idea of κόσμος as a pre-given and everlasting world,[6] which was only formed out of already existing matter, but not created in an absolute ontological sense by a subject that is external and different from that world, the Judeo-Christian tradition speaks of the world as a created thing. This faith is expressed in the doctrine of *creatio ex nihilo*.[7] We

[5] I use here the concept of ekstasis (ἔκστασις in Greek) to indicate overcoming or "getting out" of one's individual self. This particular theological connotation is based on the etymological meaning of the word, to be "displaced," "removed from one's own place," or "to stand outside" (cf. Sophocles, 1914: 443; Liddell, Scott, 1996: 520).

[6] The idea of κόσμος encompasses some important aspects of the ancient understanding of the world. It should be understood as "order," "world," but also "decoration," "ornament" and "beauty" (cf. Bychkov, 2010: 234). The concept of *kosmos* relies on the eternal order which expresses itself in perfection and harmony, being thus the criterion for both ethics and aesthetics. It also determines in the most fundamental manner the ancient cosmology and ontology.

[7] The very formulation appears in the Latin translation of the Old Testament verse "look upon Heaven and Earth, and all that is in them; and consider that God created them out of nothing, and mankind also" (2 Macc 7.28). The idea is present already in Genesis 1, although the formulation "out of nothing" does not explicitly appear. The New Testament confirms this belief, stating that everything that exists, exists because God brought it into existence and nothing is without beginning, except God (see Jn 1.1–3; cf. also Rom 4.17 and Heb 11.3). It has been developed in later theological tradition and is a commonly accepted position among the Christian theologians today. It is, however, necessary to warn that the biblical text is not

might say that the primary meaning of the doctrine, in light of the Old Testament narrative, is to underline the unconditional almightiness and absolute difference of God who gives life to everything.[8] It is also significant since it stresses the idea that God is *ontologically* free from the world; his acts of creation are free from any inner or outer necessity.[9] This leads us to another distinction between the Judeo-Christian concept of God the Creator and ancient Greek cosmology—if God is entirely free in his *ex nihilo* creation, then there is no pre-existing matter that God used to shape the world. The Creator is thus an absolute ontological *other* to created beings and is completely free in his creative activity.

This doctrine has a fundamental significance for Christian theology and theological anthropology. It shows that there is an unbridgeable ontological gap between the uncreated God and the created world, a gap that separates the *uncreated* God from the created nature of the

entirely free from formulations that indicate a creation of the world that is similar to other ancient myths, where god(s) make(s) the world out of some pre-existing matter. This "making" or "forming" of the world can be found in the book of Wisdom where the writer states "Your Almighty Hand that had made the Universe from the formless matter" (Wis 11.17). Ancient ideas of creation as forming the formless (pre-existing) matter can be found in patristic thought as well, despite the fact that they have never represented the dominant view. Following Bychkov, understanding God as the One who "brings into order" and "decorates" the ever existing matter is characteristic of Justin and Athenagoras in contrast to Tatian, Theophilus, or Tertullian. See Bychkov, 2010: 227–229. For understanding of the doctrine within the context of Hellenistic Judaism and early Christianity see May: 1978.

[8]"The doctrine of creation, then, is pre-eminently a religious affirmation about sovereignty of God and absolute dependence of the creature. To say that Yahweh made the earth is to confess that it belongs to him; he is its Lord . . . The main intention of the writer is to emphasize the absolute sovereignty of God. There is not the slightest hint that God is bound or conditioned by chaos . . ." B. W. Anderson in IDB: 728.

[9]In A. J. Torrance's characteristic words: "The doctrine of creation out of nothing emphasizes that creation is unconditioned. It denotes a radically free and sovereign act on the part of God." Torrance, 2004: 84.

world, which is a world that depends on God and finds the reason (cause) of its existence in God and his acts.

Here occurs one important link that is essential for the subsequent discussion: the capacity of creation and the capacity of freedom appear as *inseparable*. Since God is ontologically free, he is able to create out of nothing, that is, to give existence to something that never existed before. But a reverse argument would also be valid: since God creates out of nothing he is ontologically free from the world.[10]

Even from this very brief analysis of the *creatio ex nihilo* doctrine we can outline the third basic capacity of God's personal mode of existence—the capacity of creation. This doctrine makes us understand not

[10]Connecting directly the ontological freedom of God and His creative capacities raises another difficulty that requires additional explanation. The difficulty appears when we take the creation of the world to be the necessary counterpart or expression of the ontological freedom of God in principle, irrespective of the world. This connection could imply that God *must* create the world in order to be what He is, which, in turn, undermines His absolute freedom and independence from the world. This problem seems to be very difficult to solve if we approach it as an abstract, conceptual problem. However, if we approach this issue specifically from a Christian perspective, it becomes more intelligible. A typical method that Orthodox Christians employ in their understanding of sacred history as well as of dogmas is an "inverse perspective." It is quite similar to the inverse perspective that is so characteristic of Orthodox iconography. Inverse perspective in viewing theological questions and sacred history means that it is necessary to look backwards from a future point of view in order to properly understand the present and the past. This means that things can be understood only if they are viewed from an eschatological perspective, which interprets the entire history and all truths we deal with inversely in their genesis, from the end toward the beginning, and not vice versa. This ultimately means that the truth of the world, but also the truth of God, reveals itself to the human beings in Christ. Only through the person and event of Christ is God's creation both explained and justified in such a manner that it becomes the expression of His freedom and love. The freedom-necessity problem of God's creation as a manifestation of His ontological freedom is solved in Christ, who, as an ontologically free Divine Person, becomes His own creation to offer it an existence that will also be ontologically free. The issue of creation, eschatology, and "new creation" is more closely examined in chapters 2.5 and 2.6.

only creation as a capacity of God, but also the essential connection between the capacity of creation and freedom that both characterize the personal way of existence to such extent that *to be able to create* one must be *ontologically free*.

This analysis shows that God exists as a communion of Divine Persons. The essential properties of his existence, as they appear to us, are:

1. Relational nature, which means that the identity and life of each Person is constituted in a communion of love, through *ekstasis*

2. Ontological freedom

3. The capacity of creation *ex nihilo*

Can we also apply these properties to the human being as the image of God and, if so, to what extent?

1.1.2 THE IMAGE OF GOD

The point of departure for Christian anthropology is, inevitably, an *abyss*. It is the abyss that separates God and his uncreated nature from human beings and their created nature.

In contrast to God, the free Creator of everything, who exists not because of necessity but because he wills to exist, the world is not ontologically free. The world, which includes everything created, visible and invisible, does not have the cause of its existence in itself, but its cause is external—in God. Creatures depend upon the Creator, since he brought them into being both *ex nihilo* and *ex amore* (to borrow from Elizabeth Groppe) which means out of his love, so that the world, and especially human beings, can participate in his love.[11] The world then exists because God wants its existence as a whole, as well as the existence of each particular being. This means the nature of the world and all beings in it is created, and that their own nature bounds their

[11]Cf. Groppe, 2005; Moltmann, 1997.

existence. They are neither free from their nature (i.e., their created being), nor is their existence a manifestation of their freedom.

As creatures human beings participate in the necessities of created nature, sharing the same basic constraints as the rest of the world. This makes human beings fundamentally different from God.

On the other hand, humans are granted a special gift that makes them unique among the rest of the creatures: human beings are created in the "image and likeness" of God (Gen 1.26–27). This verse from the Bible describing the creation of man has produced much discussion about the exact meaning of the words "image" and "likeness" and the purpose of this distinction.[12] In the patristic literature one can find various definitions of the image of God. It seems that freedom was

[12]The two different notions used to address human similarity to God in Gen 1.26–27, the "image" and "likeness," caused extensive debate over the meaning and significance of this distinction in the early Christian literature as well as later studies. Based on the linguistic analysis of the original Hebrew terms, N. W. Porteous interprets the first concept as a "model," "picture," or "shadow." He points out that the meaning of the later term is basically the same as the first one, although he sees a possibility of interpreting the later concept as a "plan" laid before man (see Porteous, 1962: 682, 683.). In the later elaboration of these terms, the same author sees "personality" as a probable meaning of the "image," which "should not be understood in the sense of autonomous, self-legislating self of the philosophers" (ibid., 684). There is no consensus on this issue among the Fathers. It seems that Clement of Alexandria supported the idea that "image" was granted to man from the very beginning, as a part of his creation, while "likeness" is something to be achieved later, through the process of growing and becoming more perfect (see Burghardt, 1957: 3), while Gregory of Nyssa distinguishes these terms not as two different things but rather as a "static" and "dynamic" aspect of the same reality (ibid., 4). On the contrary, Athanasius and Cyril of Alexandria understand these two concepts basically as synonyms (ibid., 3, 7). The first interpretation, which points to the "likeness" as something to be achieved, is especially interesting in the context of human creativity, since it implies that man was created as an "open project" to be realized in the future, based on the potential that God had already given to him. The primary potential of man would then be the capacity to become a *person*. This would mean that the image should rise and grow to the likeness, which can only be achieved by a free activity of the person. This interpretation could also

perceived as the most common property of the image of God although one can also find other human capacities perceived as its essential properties.[13] In his analysis of the image of God, Vladimir Lossky refers to this diversity among the Fathers in their understanding the concept, claiming that the image cannot entirely be identified with any particular capacity or quality.[14] Nevertheless, he identifies the image of God in man with the human capacity to be a *person*:

> The person becomes the perfect image of God by acquiring that likeness which is the perfection of the nature common to all men. ... Made in the image of God, man is a personal being confronted with a personal God. God speaks to him as to a person, and man responds.[15]

John Zizioulas is even more resolute in the claim that the patristic thought on this issue can be summarized by pointing to personhood as the "image of God":

> Patristic theology considers the person to be an "image and likeness of God."[16]

be grounded in the fact that human freedom is in most instances interpreted as the "image" (cf. Ernst, 2009: 874, 875), which means a potential already given to man to fully be actualized in the form of likeness. Following this interpretation, it seems that from the very beginning man was envisioned as a creative being that should shape his image (identity) in such a way as to become a "god-like" being.

[13]Apart from understanding the image of God primarily as freedom, reason, and responsibility, which seems to be the most common understanding among the Fathers and other Old Testament commentators (e.g., Philo of Alexandria, Cyril of Alexandria, Basil of Caesarea, Gregory of Nyssa, Irenaeus of Lyons, Tertullian, Jerome), in the patristic literature we also find accentuation of other human capacities as essential aspects of the image of God in man, such as rationality and intelligence or memory (e.g., Augustine, Boethius). See Burghardt, 1957: 40–50; Robinson, 2011: 8–14. Cf. also McLeod, 1999: 51–85.

[14]See Lossky, 1976: 115–118.

[15]Lossky, 1976: 124.

[16]Zizioulas, 1985: 50.

If a personal way of existence (outlined in the discussion on God and identified with the very being of God) represents the image of God in man, then this image should also reflect the basic properties of the personal way of God's existence. This means that the human person should also be considered a free and creative being in communion. In contrast to equating beings with their nature (with "what they are" as a compelling existence for all created beings), the human being's personal way of existence should also imply freedom from all boundaries, including one's own nature or any pre-given fact. In its ultimate form, to exist as a person means to exist because someone wants his or her own existence to be in communion with others, and because there is also someone else who wants the existence of that particular person, for whom he or she exists as a unique and unrepeatable identity. This mode of existence is its own justification; there is not any other reason or purpose for personal existence except love that constitutes this very existence but "the goal is the person itself; personhood is the total fulfillment of being, the catholic expression of its nature."[17]

The question is how can such existence be achieved by human beings? Haven't we already said that this kind of *absolute* personhood is the exclusive property of God, who is uncreated in contrast to human beings? Can existence as freedom become reality for human beings as well?

Being made in the "image" and "likeness" of God, human beings are still a part of the created world and do not have an uncreated nature. Having in mind that the world does not have the cause of its existence in itself, the existence of all creatures is possible only through their relation to God as the giver of life. Outside this relation, creation is in permanent danger of returning to *nothingness*, which is, paradoxically, the very foundation of its being. This has a tremendous impact toward the human ability to exist as a free being, which means as a person.

[17]Zizioulas, 1985: 47.

The original necessity that human beings are confronted with comes from the character of our nature, which, in contrast to God, cannot be considered equal to human freedom. Human beings are not the origin of themselves because God brought them into being. The only way in which this initial necessity could possibly be overcome is through communion with God. This communion should be of the same quality as the communion between Divine Persons—it should be based on and expressed through love as an ecstatic existence, which overcomes particularity and isolation of individual beings. This means that human beings have a potential to become ontologically free beings, in spite of the unbridgeable distance between God and human nature, which means they are granted the possibility of existing in a way similar to the way God exists (although never in quite the same manner). Coming to this ontologically free existence (risking redundancy in this very formulation) becomes possible through overcoming the necessity of the nature and pre-given presence in general. Here we find the basic difference between exercising human and divine ontological freedom. While divine freedom is eternal and basically identical to the very being of God, human freedom is something granted to human beings as a potential which has to be actualized and achieved. This means that unlike God humans start from necessity as their point of departure in acquiring their existential freedom. They have to overcome the necessity of their own being as a pre-given circumstance, in order to enter a free existence in communion with God. This free existence should be based on freedom and love as the basic capacities of the person and the very ground of the "new creation" which is to come.

However, the initial growth of human beings in communion with God and affirmation of their personhood, which God envisioned for them, was interrupted by the Fall. The fallen existence that human beings entered after the original sin represents another basic difficulty in affirming human ontological freedom, apart from human createdness.

The essence of God's commandment "but of the tree of the knowledge of good and evil you shall not eat, for in the day you eat of it you shall surely die"[18] consists in a warning that choosing an autonomous existence is not an option for the creation. The Fall represents the failure of the original plan which God laid before man: to exist in communion with God and the rest of creation, as there cannot be existence apart from God who is its source.

The human choice of an autonomous, self-referential existence thus becomes the choice of death. This choice is a paradoxical one, since the very intention to exist apart from God is the intention to realize an impossible ontological solution.[19] Thus human beings "invented" another necessity which had not initially existed—separation and individuality as the ultimate consequences of the Fall. This was the initial choice of the human being, which turned all creatures into the *state of death*, characterized by a constant disintegration. The human quest for an autonomous life has been turned out, in its realization, to be an unintentional *quest for death*.

The question of human creation becomes especially important at this point, since the link we have established between freedom and creation tells us that if one is able to create in a genuine way, one should also be an ontologically free being. However, if creation as "bringing things into being" is not possible, then human freedom remains limited within this world and within the frame of the human pre-given nature, which means that the human being can never actually be ontologically free.

[18]Gen 2.17. Cf. Gen 3.19.

[19]Consequently, one could say that the greatest "ontological lie" from the Christian point of view is the idea that life outside God is possible. This is the reason why vanity is often considered in Christian literature the "origin of all sins." Vanity and other sins should then not be understood primarily in ethical but existential terms. They are considered sins as they lead to separation from God and thus result in a virtual, *impossible* (and yet "actual") existence.

From the foregoing analysis we can conclude that if human being is the image of God, and if this image can be identified with the personal mode of existence, then the human being should also be able to exist (1) as a being of communion that can ecstatically overcome an individual existence; (2) as an ontologically free being; and (3) as a creative being, which means as a being capable of creating, at least in some sense, out of nothing.

From the last excurses we have also seen that the human being faces two basic difficulties in the attempt to become a personal, that is, onto-logically free being. The first has to do with human createdness, and the second with the human choice of trying to establish an autonomous existence apart from God, which ends up in individuality and distance between beings.

Does this mean that the human quest for a personal existence that will be the expression of human ontological freedom, love, and the genuine ability to create is sentenced to failure? Does it mean that the image of God has only a symbolic character and should not be directly related to the very personal capacities of God? Finally, does it mean that the highest expression of human creative capacities is to be found only in the production of artworks and beautiful objects, which means that they cannot play any other role in Christian anthropology?

As we have also seen, creation in its absolute meaning, as "bring-ing things into being," remained in the patristic literature an exclusive capacity of God. Understanding human creative (in)capacities in most of Christian tradition can be described by the famous remark that *crea-tura non potest creare*.[20] Those (in)capacities were appreciated mainly through the prism of theological aesthetics, focusing on a theological justification of art as a means of transmitting beauty and a theological message to the faithful.[21]

---

[20]"The creature cannot create." Cf. Pope, 2005: 45.

[21]One can, however, occasionally find references to "creativity" as a part of the

1.2 The Role of Creativity in John Zizioulas' Anthropology

I shall begin the analysis of human creative capacities and their relation to artistic practice by critical examination of John Zizioulas' argument on human creativity. Contrary to the traditional perception of
human creativity, Zizioulas argues that the human being is a *creative*
being, which means a being capable of creation by "bringing things into
being."[22] The idea that the human being can create *ex nihilo*, implies
that this creation is not only one among many human faculties, but
a distinct capacity with serious ontological consequences. I use the
adjective "*ex nihilo*" here to stress the noun "creation" as a genuine act
or "bringing things into being" in contrast to "creation" as merely giving objects a new and, presumably, beautiful form.

As I pointed out in the beginning, Nikolai Berdyaev was also a
prominent Orthodox author who addressed the concept of human creation in a similar manner, stating that "each creative act is in its essence
creation out of nothing."[23] Unlike Zizioulas, who faces the problem of
the pre-given matter as an obstacle in human creative attempts, as we
shall see below, Berdyaev clearly states that human creation *ex nihilo*

image of God in man and, thus, a capacity which also belongs to the human being
in a basic way. Georges Florovsky notes in this respect that Gregory of Nyssa speaks
of language as an example of human creative faculty: "Gregory sees language as a
product of man's creativity. The 'invention' of language by man was not arbitrary or
capricious but was accomplished through the natural faculty of reason. . . . 'Man's
faculty or potential for language is the work of our Creator.' Man can realize this
potential in a free and creative way. . . . Language, sounds, and the conceptions they
express are all created by men through the divinely bestowed faculty of 'invention,'
ἐπίνοια. . . . Invention is the creative power of thought, a 'more exhaustive analysis
of the object of thought.' . . . In attempting to define the common element between
the name and its object, Gregory proposes that this connection is established by the
free and creative faculty of the intellect. Names are invented for things and united
to them but they do not arise from things." Florovsky, 1987: 165–166.

[22]Zizioulas, 1975: 411.
[23]Berdyaev, 1996-a, Vol. I: 106.

does not mean the absence of matter but "an absolute gain, which is not determined by anything."[24] He also connects freedom and creativity in the most direct way, saying that the "secret of creativity is the secret of freedom."[25]

Both authors see artistic creation as a manifestation of human creative capacities par excellence. Berdyaev states that artistic creation "best represents the essence of the creative act," while "art is primarily the field of creation."[26] Zizioulas speaks of art as a "genuine creation"[27] and considers creativity a concept which is "significantly applied to Art par excellence, though we seldom appreciate the real implications of this for theology and anthropology."[28]

In contrast to early Patristic literature where art (i.e., the visual arts) was perceived essentially as a way of making things beautiful by means of human skills, the field of art becomes here the field of human authentic creation and even *ex nihilo* creation, acquiring a more prominent position within Orthodox Christian ontology and anthropology than it ever had before.

Unlike Berdyaev, who had no interest in making a strict theological argument, Zizioulas formulates a very articulate theological position in this respect. Discussing human creative capacities manifested in the arts, Zizioulas situates human capacities in the broader context of his theology of personhood. In order to understand the full anthropological implications of Zizioulas' argument on creativity I will give a brief explanation of his understanding of "personhood" as an ontological category.

---

[24]Berdyaev, 1996-a, Vol. I: 119.

[25]Berdyaev, 1996-a, Vol. I: 119.

[26]Berdyaev, 1996-a, Vol. II: 45.

[27]"Art as genuine creation, and not as a representational rendering of reality, is nothing other than an attempt by man to affirm his presence in a manner free from the 'necessity' of existence." Zizioulas, 1985: 42, fn. 38.

[28]Zizioulas, 1975: 412.

1.2.1 PERSONHOOD AS THE CONCEPTUAL FRAMEWORK FOR ZIZIOULAS' ARGUMENT ON CREATIVITY

As we have already seen, the concept of "person" has been employed to explain the existence of God, or more concretely to explain how the Christian God is at the same time one and three, the Trinity. Zizioulas, however, radicalizes this personal dimension in the case of the human being, building an entire ontology and theology on personhood as the image of God.

The roots of Zizioulas' "personalism" lie primarily in Russian theology and religious philosophy and in contemporaneous Western philosophy of the past century.[29]

Zizioulas, however, seems to be more radical in his "personalism." He is a theologian who distinguishes quite sharply between the concepts of "individuality" and "personhood." In his view, these two concepts are opposite in their meaning. The former implies separation between beings and the ability to identify particular beings with *what they are*, as monads. This state is the consequence of the fall. The latter concept is a new mode of existence, which represents, as we have seen, the image of God. This distinction can be seen in an interesting example by Zizioulas. He speaks of our physical body as one of the most remarkable manifestations of individuality. The body represents our "biological hypostasis" which "is 'constituted' by a man's conception and birth."[30] It bears a strong sign of individuality but it also shows some traces of its personal designation. Human beings try to realize this

[29]The person-individual distinction could appear in Zizioulas' work under the influence of Jacques Maritain, Nikolai Berdyaev and Martin Buber (see Zizioulas, 2001; Turcescu, 2002). The profound influence of Jean-Paul Sartre's existentialism and Martin Heidegger's philosophy on Zizioulas' thought is also evident. For Lossky-Zizioulas relations, including both similarities and differences in their theology (particularly in their Trinitarian theology) see Papanikolaou, 2006.

[30]Zizioulas, 1985: 50.

personal dimension of the body through the movements toward others, that the body can perform (e.g., in an effort to communicate). But this intention remains unsuccessful, since the very means with which one is trying to bring it about (one's body) prevents one from doing so. This shows the individual character of body in the fallen state:

> Constitutionally the hypostasis is inevitably tied to the natural instinct, to an impulse which is 'necessary' and not subject to the control of freedom. . . . As a result it does not have the power to affirm its hypostasis with absolute ontological freedom . . . The body, which is born as a biological hypostasis, behaves like the fortress of ego, like a new 'mask' which hinders the hypostasis from becoming a person, that is, from affirming itself as love and freedom. The body tends towards the person but leads finally to the individual. . . . All this means that man as a biological hypostasis is intrinsically a tragic figure. . . . His body is the tragic instrument which leads to communion with others, stretching out a hand, creating language, speech, conversation, art, kissing. But at the same time it is the 'mask' of hypocrisy, the fortress of individualism, the vehicle of the final separation, death.[31]

Not only human beings, but all creatures and the totality of the created world, are also affected by individuality. On the one hand, the world is a necessary presence for humans and the reason for that lies in the very nature of all creatures—human beings did not (and actually could not) participate in creation of the world or of themselves. On the other hand, this compelling presence (existence which is not the result of freedom) is strengthened through the Fall. Individuality signifies not only a distance between God and human being; it also signifies the distance between beings in the world.

[31]Zizioulas, 1985: 50–52.

The necessities that bound human beings, as well as the whole world, are not final and irreparable in the view of Orthodox theology. In the fallen state human beings still do not lose the image of God, according to which they were originally created. The possibility for the actualization of human personhood and affirmation of the personal mode of existence over the individual one, Zizioulas finds in the "ecclesial hypostasis" as opposed to the "biological hypostasis." The ecclesial hypostasis is also Zizioulas' solution to the problem of human ontological freedom.

In *Being as Communion* Zizioulas explains the distinction between the biological and ecclesial hypostasis. The biological hypostasis is the primary "identity" of the human being, which everyone carries from birth. It bears a strong mark of individuality since the very way in which human beings come to this world is marked by individualization and separation.[32] This state of individualism and death can be overcome only in the ecclesial hypostasis. This hypostasis characterizes "newly born" persons, those who, through baptism are "born from above," becoming members of a new (coming) reality— the Church.

> The first and the most important characteristic of the Church is that she brings man into a kind of relationship with the world which is not determined by the laws of biology. Thus a characteristic of the ecclesial hypostasis is the capacity of the person to love without exclusiveness, and to do this not out of conformity with a moral commandment ... but out of his 'hypostatic constitution', out of the fact that his new birth from the womb of the Church has made him part of a network of relationships which

[32]"Every man who comes into the world bears his 'hypostasis,' which is not entirely unrelated to love: he is the product of a communion between two people. ... But this biological constitution of man's hypostasis suffers radically from two 'passions' which destroy precisely that towards which the human hypostasis is thrusting, namely the person. The first 'passion' is what we may call 'ontological' necessity." Zizioulas, 1985: 50.

transcends every exclusiveness. . . . The ecclesial hypostasis exists historically in this manner as a confirmation of man's capacity not to be reduced to his tendency to become a bearer of individuality, separation and death. The ecclesial hypostasis is the *faith* of man in his capacity to become a person and his *hope* that he will indeed become an authentic person. In other words it is faith and hope in the immortality of man as a person.[33]

Further explication of this issue leads Zizioulas to point to the future, to the Kingdom of God as the eschatological reality in which the ecclesial hypostasis exists. The historical appearance of the coming Kingdom of God can be found in the Eucharist. The Eucharist is the icon of the "things to come," and makes the reality that is to come (in the future) already present "here" and "now."

Salvation then means that human beings are liberated from the necessity of individual existence, which is death-bearing as it is manifested primarily through the mutual separation of beings. However, salvation also means that human beings are, at least partially, liberated from the necessity of their nature, which has no ground apart from God's love. Salvation is offered in the "new birth," that is in the Church as Christ's body, which iconizes the Heavenly Kingdom as an eschatological reality. Thus the foundation of our new hypostases (persons) becomes love, not biological necessity. It is love which constitutes the Church— God's love for his people and the whole creation, as well as human love for God and the rest of the world which becomes a eucharistic (thanksgiving) oblation offered to God. Following this approach, human beings can exist in a way similar to God as their existence becomes constituted upon this new foundation. They live a new existence, not because it is a driving force of their nature that they must obey, as in biological birth or death, but because it is the result of their freedom and love. This movement that human beings make in the

[33]Zizioulas, 1985: 56–58.

course of history, within the visible Church, is of course only an icon of what is to be completed in the *eschaton*.

We can conclude that for Zizioulas the ecclesial hypostasis, in its eschatological perspective, appears as a solution to all the necessities that human beings face. However the question of the significance and possibility of human creation remains open. In the following chapter I will analyze Zizioulas' argument on creativity and the link he establishes between creativity, human existence, and artistic production. Based on this, I will present questions that I intend to explore in the further analysis.

The foregoing analysis shows Zizioulas' perspective on the root of the problem of human existence as well as the solution. Zizioulas sees personhood as the only way to salvation, primarily because being a person necessarily implies an ecclesial and eucharistic dimension.

This is the framework in which Zizioulas develops his argument on creativity. We will consider now the role of human creative capacities in Zizioulas' personalism.

1.2.2 ZIZIOULAS' ARGUMENT ON CREATIVITY

The key text in which Zizioulas deals with the problem of human creativity is his 1975 article on "Human Capacity and Incapacity." I will quote here the full, albeit long passage, in which Zizioulas discusses human creative capacities, drawing at the same time important conclusions regarding human presence in the world and the tension between individuality and personhood.

> It would seem, therefore, that the identification of hypostasis with Person—this historic cross-fertilisation between Greek and biblical thought that took place in the fourth century – has ultimately served to show that the notion of Person is to be found only in God and that human personhood is never satisfied with itself until

it becomes in this respect an *imago Dei*. This is the greatness and tragedy of man's personhood and nothing manifests this more clearly than a consideration of his capacity and incapacity, especially from an ontological point of view. We can see this by considering one of the most important capacities of human personhood, namely *creating*: man is capable of creating, of bringing things into being. When we employ the terms 'creation', 'creating' or 'creativity' in relation to personhood, we must not have in mind the idea of 'manufacturing' with which we usually associate man's ability to be a creator. Admirable as it may be, man's capacity to manufacture and produce useful objects even of the highest quality, such as the machines or our modern technological civilisation, is not to be directly associated with human Personhood. Perhaps on this point the contrast we have been making here between man as a Person on the one hand and man as an individual thinking or acting agent on the other hand, becomes more evident. The 'creation' of a machine requires man's individualization both in terms of his *seizing, controlling and dominating* reality, i.e., turning beings into things, and also in terms of *combination* of human individuals in a collective effort, i.e., of turning man himself into a thing, an instrument and a means to an end. . . . But when we say that man is capable of creating *by being a person*, we imply something entirely different, and that has to do with a double possibility which this kind of creation opens up. On the one hand, 'things' or the world around acquire a 'presence' as an integral and relevant part of the totality of existence, and on the other hand man himself becomes 'present' as a unique and unrepeatable hypostasis of being and not as an impersonal number in a combined structure. In other words, in this way of understanding creating, the movement is from thinghood to personhood and not the other way around. This is, for example, what happens in the case of a work of real art as contrasted to a machine. When we look at a painting or listen to music we have in front of us 'the beginning of a world', a 'presence' in which 'things' and substances (cloth, oil, etc.) or qualities (shape, color, etc.) or sounds become part of a personal presence. And this is entirely the achievement of Personhood, a distinctly unique capacity of man, which, unlike other technological achievements, is not threatened by the emerging intelligent beings of computer science. The term 'creativity' is significantly applied to Art par excellence, though we seldom appreciate the real implications of this for theology and anthropology.[34]

From this extraordinary passage we learn that (1) creativity is a basic property of the human person, (2) art production is the manifestation of human creativity par excellence, and (3) a person is capable of demonstrating his or her own personal presence in works of art.

Although Zizioulas does not explicitly call the human capacity of creation a capacity of creation *ex nihilo*, it is clear that he refers to some kind of ontologically free creation: he makes a clear distinction between "creation" and "manufacture"—the first is "bringing things into being," the second is merely transformation and utilization of the world and matter that is already there. (In *Being as Communion* Zizioulas is even more explicit: "Genuine art is not simply creation on the basis of something which already exists, but a tendency towards creation ex nihilo."[35]) We find creation in art, because there, in art production as it is colloquially assumed, we see a personal presence, "the beginning of a world," in contrast to the crafts or technical labor, which show an individualized mode of existence.

Following Zizioulas' argument further, we find out that this capacity of human personal presence in artworks is finally manifested as "absence" in which the "tragedy" of human existence can be seen:

[34]Zizioulas, 1975: 410–412.
[35]Zizioulas, 1985: 42, fn. 38.

Now, this possibility of 'presence', which is implied in human personhood, reveals at the same time the tragic incapacity which is intrinsic in this very capacity of personhood. This is to be seen in the paradoxical fact that the presence of being in and through the human person is ultimately revealed as an absence. . . . If we take again our example from the world of art, the fundamental thing that we must observe with regard to the 'presence' it creates, is that the artist himself is absent. This is not an entirely negative statement. The tragedy lies in the fact that it is at once positive and negative: the artist exists for us only because he is absent. Had we not had his work (which points to his absence), he would not exist for us or for the world around, even if we had heard of him or seen him; he is by not being there (an incidental actual presence of the artist next to us while we are looking at his work would add nothing to his real presence in and through his work, which remains a pointer to his absence). . . .

In so far, therefore, as the human person is an entity whose being or particularity is realized by way of a transcendence of its boundaries in an event of communion, its personhood reveals itself as *presence*. But in so far as the human person is a being whose particularity is established *also* by its boundaries (a body), personhood realizes this presence as *absence*. Since both of these have their focus on one and the same entity, they represent a paradox, the two components of which must be maintained *simultaneously*, if justice is to be done to the mystery of human personhood. . . . The presence-in-absence paradox is, therefore, inevitable in a consideration of man as person, particularly from the point of view of his capacity to be a creator.[36]

Turning back to the creation of art as the best illustration of the presence-in-absence paradox, Zizioulas comes to the root of the

[36]Zizioulas, 1975: 412–415.

problem. He contrasts a personal mode of existence with "being" as a "given datum of ontology"[37] (as in the ancient Greek ontology, for instance). From a Christian perspective the problem is approached from quite the opposite direction, since the person, especially in the case of God, has ontological supremacy over being or essence. Applied to the human being, this ontology reveals the limitations of man and the reasons for the "presence-in-absence" paradox which characterizes human creation:

> The fact that presence in and through personhood is revealed to man in the form of absence constitutes a sign *par excellence* of the *creaturely* limitation of humanity. The idea of *creatio ex nihilo* was employed by the Fathers in order to oppose the Greek view of a creation of the world out of pre-existing matter. At first sight it may not seem quite clear why this idea is so significant for illustrating the difference between being an uncreated creator and being a creator as creature, but it becomes evident that it is so, as soon as we look at it anthropologically rather than simply and primarily cosmologically and theologically. In this particular case, in which as I have argued the mystery of personhood is at stake, creating out of pre-existing matter implies the distance (*diastēma*) due to what we call space and time, i.e., categories indicating a relational event by emphasizing simultaneously unity and distance, i.e., absence and presence, or rather presence-in-absence. The characteristic of creatures, as contrasted with God, lies precisely in this distance which accounts for their multiplicity: creatures are not one, but, taking all together, many and diverse because they are divided up in separated places (Athanasius). The limitation of creaturehood lies in this 'distance' which makes the creatures 'comprehensible' and 'containable' (*chōrēta*). Space and time, when viewed from the angle of the nature of creaturehood, are two terms which reveal a

[37]Zizioulas, 1975: 416.

relationship of separateness (*chōrismos*) and hence of individual-ization; only when they are viewed from the angle of personhood do these terms reveal a relationship of unity (*katholou*) and hence of communion. Thus personhood, when applied strictly to crea-tures, results in a contradiction between the *katholou* and the *kata meros*. And since personhood affirms the integrity and catholic-ity of being (cf. *hypostasis*) and must of necessity overcome the distance of individualization (cf. *ekstasis*), being a person implies, existentially speaking, the frustration of the contradiction between presence and absence. This frustration would not have existed had there not been the spatio-temporal roots of creaturehood, i.e., in the last analysis, *beginning*. Thus the fact that the artist is absent through his personal presence in his work is due primarily to the fact that he has used pre-existing matter, because this means that his personal presence is embodied in something that is already part of the space-time structure which makes it something contain-able (*chōrēton*) and thus present only by being distant from other things. Had God done the same thing, i.e., used pre-existing mat-ter, he would be caught in the same predicament and his presence in his creation would be a presence in absence for him—something that would rule out entirely the possibility of a presence without absence.[38]

This passage shows the tremendous significance of human creative capacities in understanding and actualizing our existence. Creativity becomes a capacity which shows the *mode* of existence and the very possibility of a personal being. Art becomes a testimony to the human being's tragic but very basic quest: to become a person within the boundaries of this world. In light of our analysis of the very concept of person, it becomes clear that in ontological terms the task facing the human being is to transfigure his or her self from an existence where

[38]Zizioulas, 1975: 416–418.

nature has priority, to a Godlike existence, in which personhood has the ontological priority. The fundamental means to achieve this transformation are to be found in the human capacity to be the image of God, to escape individuality in an ecstatic and free act. To give ontological priority to personhood over nature requires an act of "new creation" in which the existence of creatures is not subjected to necessity (pre-given presence) but is the result of a free decision. This Godlike existence is constituted in a manner similar to God's existence—human beings exist not because their existence is a necessity into which they have been cast, but because they *want* their existence in communion with God. Instead of nature or essence, freedom and *ekstasis* become the "foundation" (*hypostasis*) of both God's and humanity's existence.

We might ask at this point what the possible role of art is in this existential attempt of the human being. So far, we have seen that through creative activities, the human being shows the quest for presence, but in Zizioulas' view this is a tragic attempt, since it results in the "presence-in-absence" paradox. However, Zizioulas sees the significance of art precisely in the demonstration of the human capacity to be(come) *person*:

> The significance of art . . . lies in that it shows that Man as a person is not content with the presence of beings as they are given to him in the world. . . . it means that Personhood prefers to create its presence as absence rather than be contained, comprehended, described and manipulated through the circumscribability and individualization which are inherent in all creaturehood. Personhood thus proves to be *in* this world—through man—but not *of* this world.[39]

[39]Zizioulas, 1975: 420. For Vladimir Lossky art is even more significant. He claims that "personality can only be grasped in this life by a direct intuition; it can only be expressed in a work of art. When we say 'this is by Mozart' or 'this is by Rembrandt' we are in both cases dealing with a personal world which has no equivalent

It becomes clear from the above quoted passage that Zizioulas takes the capacity of creation as illustrating the human desire to become a person even within the boundaries of this world—which becomes an unsuccessful attempt, a *tragic* failure. In this tragic *absence*, as a result of the person's unsuccessful quest for presence, human capacity is revealed to be a person. But if this is the ultimate destiny of the human being in this world, then it seems that we have learned nothing more about the human person than we could learn from ancient Greek tragedy.[40] In both cases we witness to human attempts to escape the necessity of this world and to cross its boundaries. In both cases this attempt is unsuccessful; they just point to the human being as a tragic figure whose

anywhere." Lossky, 1976: 53. Unfortunately, Lossky does not develop this point any further. It is, for example, not very clear why this awareness of a personal identity/presence in front of a painting by Rembrandt (expressed with the phrase 'this is by Rembrandt') is different from the awareness of a personal identity ("personality") in front of a hat or a walking stick that belonged to Rembrandt. How is it different from looking at a scarf that belonged to a person we knew and were attached to?

[40]And I refer here to Zizioulas' interpretation of tragedy he offers in *Being as Communion*: "The theater, and tragedy in particular, is the setting in which the conflicts between human freedom and the rational necessity of a unified and harmonious world, as they were understood by the ancient Greeks, are worked out in dramatic form. It is precisely in the theater that man strove to become a 'person,' to rise up against this harmonious unity which oppresses him as rational and moral necessity. It is there that he fights with gods and with his fate; it is there that he sins and transgresses; but it is there too that he constantly learns—according to the stereotyped principle of ancient tragedy—that he can neither escape fate ultimately, not continue to show hubris to the gods without punishment, nor sin without suffering the consequences. ... His freedom is circumscribed, or rather there is no freedom for him—since a 'circumscribed freedom' would be a contradiction in terms—and consequently his 'person' is nothing but a 'mask,' something which has no bearing on his true 'hypostasis,' something without ontological content. ... But together with this aspect there is also another, namely, that as a result of this mask man—the actor, but properly also the spectator—has acquired a certain taste of freedom, a certain specific 'hypostasis,' a certain identity, which the rational and moral harmony of the world in which he lives denies him. ... But as a result of the mask he has become a person, albeit for a brief period ..." Zizioulas, 1985: 31–33.

personhood reveals itself in the tragic ending.[41] The only solution in such a situation can be found in the *eschaton*, in the end of "this world," which also brings the end of necessity. This is where, in Zizioulas' view, the existential problems of the human being can finally be solved and where the personal identity of each human being can be fully revealed and justified. Within the boundaries of history and the fallen state, the human being is unable to escape this tragedy.

Despite the fact that eschatology is the only final Christian answer to the problem of history and "this world" in general, it seems to me that we should try to find some additional answers as to the role and significance of human creation. Otherwise, the position of human beings in the ancient Greek and Christian view of history becomes very similar,

[41]If we perceive human position in this world as a tragic one, since human freedom cannot fully be actualized in this world of necessities, it becomes unclear what is the difference between the understanding of the human being, as it appears in Zizioulas' interpretation of the tragedy, and Zizioulas' own perception of the human being in his/her "tragic" attempt to create? It seems that the apparent difference lies in the reasons of the human's tragic position in the world as well as in the ethical implications of that position. The ancient tragedy might point to the personal dimension of the human being and the human quest for an ontological freedom. However, heroes from the Greek tragedies suffer because they tried to cross the boundaries of the pre-given world. Their rebellion against the necessity of the everlasting order (cosmos) and its laws must, therefore, be punished. The ethical lesson that has to be learned from the tragedy as well as from the basic aesthetical principles is that the world in its totality, together with its laws, is *good* and *beautiful* (which is summarized in the maxims of the oracle in Delphi). Therefore disobedience to the everlasting laws and the faith representing this world must be punished to preserve the harmony of the universe and to give an ethical lesson that living a *good* life is possible only in accord with the everlasting (universal) natural and ethical laws. On the contrary, the lesson that the Christians might read from the same stories is that although unsuccessful in their attempt to realize ontological freedom within the boundaries of this world, the effort of "breaking the rules" is exactly what makes these tragic figures human in the deepest possible sense. Their tragedy becomes their victory, a triumph over the world of necessity, independent of the fact that their quest for freedom does not find its final solution within the boundaries of history.

perhaps dangerously so, except in the eschatological perspective which represents the hope of Christians that the necessity of this world does not have final say over the human being.

Apart from this issue, we face another problem when trying to determine more specifically in what the human creation *ex nihilo* consists. If we understand the human's genuine ability to create as primarily the creation of matter, we face a difficulty in the fact that human beings are still unable to create matter out of nothing. If one is forced always to use pre-existing matter in order to create, it seems self-evident that this creation cannot be *ex nihilo*. Reasoning this way seems to be in complete accordance with Zizioulas' conclusions as to the presence-in-absence paradox. This brings us back to the question: If human ontological freedom can realistically exist within history, can it be realized, either in history or in the *eschaton*, without threatening the absolute ontological difference between God and the human being?

If we try to find out what human genuine creation means for Zizioulas, putting aside the obvious inability of the human being to produce matter, two possible solutions emerge. One solution is to look at human genuine creation as something consisting precisely in different particular, specific, and unrepeatable forms that human beings produce when acting as creators (e.g., in the arts). In other words, to quote Aristotle Papanikolaou: "To create as a person is to imbue the created object with the uniqueness and irreducibility of the person."[42] In contrast to creation understood in this way, "manufacture" would be the potentially endless reproduction of the same forms. This explanation points to an important aspect of the human–world relation. It is a link between one's particular and unrepeatable identity and the way in which this identity is manifested in the world, in the production of objects that have unique forms. Things formed in a unique manner start, consequently, to witness to their creator, bearing the signs of the unrepeatable identity

[42]Papanikolaou, 2006: 143.

of the author. However, we face a difficulty here when we try to explain how this would be authentic or genuine creation. First of all, the pre-given matter appears not only as a necessity which causes human presence in absence; it paradoxically becomes the necessary condition of the human creation one must use to demonstrate one's unique personal identity. In order to avoid the obvious contradiction, we have to frame the capacity of genuine creation as reshaping the pre-given material in an original way, leaving a personal seal on one's work. Although this explains how the human person becomes materially manifested in the world in his or her uniqueness, it becomes difficult to determine what would be a specific or unrepeatable character of such creations (e.g., artworks).[43] Is it, for instance, a specific expression of the artist's individual character, such as one's emotions, that we observe in the gestures left on the canvas? The problem with this concept, which so remarkably resembles modern ideas about the artist as a talented and extraordinary individual, is that it is culturally and historically rooted in the post-Renaissance ("Western") understanding of the artistic creation as producing something "original," "inspired," and "beautiful." The real difficulty lies in the possibility of linking the individual character of artwork that someone makes with his or her specific psychophysical characteristics. We are thus in danger of suggesting that human creation is a reflection of the individual's psychophysical characteristics and potential, with no obvious connection to human personhood, as defined above. On a very elementary level, it could be said that human creative works become basically similar to someone's signature or fingerprints, because they also bear testimony to the particular (specific, distinctive) character of a concrete human being. Although this aspect

[43]One reason for that we find in Papanikolaou's critical response to Lucian Turcescu's reading of Zizioulas' concept of personhood: "For Zizioulas, uniqueness is identified with 'irreplaceability'. A particular embodiment of a combination of qualities . . . does not contribute to uniqueness or irreplaceability." Papanikolaou, 2004: 603.

has been one element, if not indeed the crucial element of artworks in their relation to the unique identity of "creative individuals" in modern times, it becomes problematic for one main reason: it allows us to speak of human creation without connecting it to the ontological freedom of the human being. It actually becomes possible to separate the question of creation, which can then be reduced to the recognition of the specific aesthetic properties of the created object, from the question of ontological freedom (if we want to avoid the simple conclusion that the human being cannot be an ontologically free being). Giving a specific, particular seal to human works can, for example, be explained psychoanalytically, which does not necessarily require a theological foundation for the argument. On the other hand, looking from a positivistic perspective, human creativity could be reduced to the complex web of various physical and chemical factors that impose a behavior we call "creativity," although it does not represent any ontologically free activity of humans. We could, moreover, imagine artificial intelligence of future generations that could produce endless variations of forms, without a personal identity motivating the process. Finally, human creative capacities appear in all these solutions as separated from the very basic features of the human person as being in communion. Within this perspective, creativity becomes a property of the individual but it is not directly related by any means to the act of communion. In short, I think that human beings can leave traces of their specific identity in the form of material objects, but this does not necessarily lead to their ontological freedom or, at least, their connection to ontological freedom is unclear.

The other solution would be to admit the human incapacity to create *ex nihilo* within the course of history, given the necessity of the human created nature, individual existence in history, and the necessary presence of the pre-given matter in the world. We could, consequently, conclude that this human incapacity to create is limited to history but it may eventually be manifested as a personal capacity in the *eschaton*. This presumes that everything and everyone will be transformed in the *eschaton* to such extent that presence of everything will not be a necessity for the human being any more. In such a situation, even pre-existing matter will not be a pre-given condition, but a presence "out of love." (This solution is attractive for various reasons and I will return to it in the concluding chapter of this study.) The difficulty with this solution is that we are then in a danger of denying an inherent connection between history, together with human creative activities in it, and eschatology. Human creative attempts become something without real existence in history; it becomes impossible to achieve or manifest them "here" and "now," but they appear as something *only* hoped for, that will eventually take place in the coming world.

To find a satisfactory solution to the problem of human creation *ex nihilo,* which in my view has to be maintained as a human potential that appears not only in eschatology but also somehow in history, we should approach human creation in a different way. We have to ask if human creation *ex nihilo* primarily and necessarily means the production of matter out of nothing. Can an act that is not the creation of matter itself be meaningfully called creation *ex nihilo* and on what basis?

In answering these questions I obviously take a different approach compared to the ways in which the concept of creation *ex nihilo* has traditionally been understood. I return here to the analogy between the creative acts of the biblical God and the work of the Greek Demiurge. Human transformation of the pre-given matter (even with a personal seal) functions as the image of the Demiurge, who does not really produce matter but just gives it form, potentially an infinite number of different forms. In a Christian understanding of the human being, however, the human person is not the image of the Demiurge but of the Creator of heaven and earth.

In order to understand properly the question of whether the human being can create in spite of the presence of the pre-given matter, this question should be related to God's creation as its prototype. We should examine the function of the *ex nihilo* idea in the Judeo-Christian tradition in order to see if the idea can perform the same or a similar function within the context of the human being.

As was pointed out earlier, the writer of the biblical narrative was not concerned with abstract questions such as, "What is this 'nothing' out of which creation appears?" or "Does this 'nothing' exist parallel to God prior to the creation?" and so forth. The main purpose was to underline God's absolute freedom in his creative work and the gap separating God and his creatures as substantially different realities. Consequently, freedom becomes this "nothing" out of which creation appears. The fact that God is free from any necessity makes this creation "groundless." His freedom and love appear as the cause of creation.

If we apply the same logic to the human creation, we can formulate the thesis in this way: If human beings can be free from the ontological necessities they face in this world and their existence in it (which is a constraining factor for them, in difference to God), they are also able to create *ex nihilo*. Thus, the problem of human creation becomes the problem of the possibility of human ontological freedom in this world.

Following this path the question of human capacity or incapacity to produce matter itself becomes of secondary importance, since the problem of human ontological freedom would not be solved even if human beings could, with help of a very advanced technology for instance, produce matter out of nothing. If human beings, at some point, become able to make particles of matter appear out of *nothing*, this newly created matter would still be distanced from them, still representing a compelling presence. Such creation would not be an expression of human ontological freedom and love by itself. The problem thus cannot be solved outside the human being and the very ontological status of human beings in their createdness has to be clarified.

Therefore, human (in)ability to be free and to create can only be solved at this level.

One of the first questions that has to be explored is related to the problem of pre-given matter as the basic necessity that every human attempt to create is confronted with. Is the pre-given matter the *sine qua non* for human creation *ex nihilo*? Can the human being overcome the boundaries of the created world via creative activity in history and how does such activity relate to eschatology?

Bearing in mind the problem of individuality and the ecclesial dimension of human existence, which in Zizioulas' view is the only way to overcome individuality, it is also necessary to examine whether human creation might be a relevant concept in constituting the ecclesial hypostasis. Is there, in other words, an ecclesial significance of the creative act? Given the fact that the Church (i.e., Eucharist) is the means of human salvation, I will also address the question of a potential soteriological significance of human creation. The vital aspect of this issue, in light of the previous analysis of human personhood, is the question of whether or not the transformation from an individual to person can take place via a creative act as well.

The examples from modern and contemporary art practices I employ in my analysis help us in understanding human creativity and in formulating a theologically significant argument as to human creative capacities. Having expressed my presumption that the human being can create *ex nihilo*, my preliminary hypothesis in this respect is that human creative capacities do have the potential of overcoming both the state of necessity and individuality, bringing the human being to an ontologically free existence. This means that it is possible to find a solution for the basic difficulties that Zizioulas observed regarding the human (in)capacity to create. This, however, requires a somewhat modified understanding of the relationship between human existence in history, human creativity, and the eschatological reality.

CHAPTER 2

Creation and Presence

In this chapter I address the problem of the pre-given presence and individuality as, following Zizioulas, two main obstacles in the human attempt to create *ex nihilo*. I will first focus on the problem of pre-given matter and analyze the extent to which this can be considered the *sine qua non* condition of human creativity. In order to construct my argument that human genuine creation is realistic in spite of the presence of pre-given matter and the state of individuality, I will analyze three types of examples from twentieth-century art that, in my view, help us to theologically appreciate human creativity.

In the second part of this chapter I address the issue of individuality and the human *natural* (and therefore compelling) presence in this world as the second basic difficulty which the human being faces when trying to create.

Finally, I examine human creativity and freedom with respect to time, the *eschaton* and the "new creation."

2.1 Theological Significance of Artistic Practice

In the previous chapter we saw that the question of human creation cannot be analyzed apart from the human capacity for freedom. This is so because the ability to create has to be recognized as a basic capacity of the human person if freedom, as a substantial aspect of the image of God in man, is to make sense on an ontological level. We also saw that individuality and personhood can be explained as two different ontologies, modes of existence, or approaches to the human-world relation. Individuality signifies acceptance of the pre-given state (necessity) in the fallen world, while the concept of personhood reflects the possibility the human being has to change his or her way of existence, transforming it from the state of necessity into existence as freedom.

These two ontologies define two different types of relations to the pre-given presence of the world, including matter as a necessary presence. The relation toward the world, which is based on individuality, is marked by the human choice to exist as a *thing* in the world. Individuality, in this sense, represents basic human equality to other created beings in the world (including inert entities) and human willingness to identify with his or her createdness. Therefore the pre-given presence of things in the world is not only one among many necessities that the human being tries to overcome. The pre-given presence becomes the primary ontology of the human being in the fallen state, based on the choice to live an individual existence. The human being, identified with his or her individuality and nature, has a presence in history that confirms the decision to break the relationship with God, which led to the Fall. As a result, the personal way of existence, although still present as a possibility, virtually disappears from the human horizon. Human beings become what they choose to be—things and facts of an objectivized and naturalized world, with no unmediated part in the life of God, except through the icon. Since human beings identified their existence with their being as creatures, whose real base or hypostasis outside of communion with God is *nothing*, they chose non-existence to be the foundation of their existence. This fact makes humanity's existence in history a double paradox. This fact caused human beings and the rest of the creatures to exist *as* a process of permanent dying and disintegration. Instead of a communion of love as the only affirmation of existence, everything turns into a state of mutual hostility and destruction. Things in the world become alien to the human being and each creature. This can be illustrated by the necessity to kill and eat other living beings to be able to survive, which makes our biological hypostasis able to survive and flourish until it also becomes food for other creatures.[1]

In such a situation, the only possible human relation to the things in the world is of an individual nature. This means that man can size, re-shape, and utilize things and matter in the world, as they also exist as a necessity for him. This rootedness of the human individual's

[1]This fact is very telling indeed. Human life in the fallen state can only be sustained by the consumption and death of other beings, through the act of eating. This is the most obvious manifestation of human attempt to build his or her individual existence on the basis of the created nature, without God. A human being tries to secure his or her existence by continuously internalizing death. This shows the initial human choice to make nothingness the very ground of human existence. Paradoxically enough, one does it to sustain life. In the end, an individual as a biological hypostasis really becomes what human beings chose to be—nothing, ending up in disintegration and death while becoming food for other creatures. Here Orthodox Christian fasting appears as bearing an ontologically different approach to life. Here we see that fasting, as an integral part of the liturgical life, becomes a "new philosophy of life." Through fasting one refuses to equalize his/her existence with the death of other creatures. In fasting, which requires a free and willing decision to restrict the consumption of food and other products (both qualitatively and quantitatively) as well as to reduce human needs in general (through, for example, "spiritual fasting"), human beings choose to ground their life primarily on the relation with God. This is marked by insisting on prayer as an integral part of fasting, which is a commonplace in the entire Orthodox tradition. It is also not by chance that love in the Orthodox Christian tradition has been considered the final purpose of fasting. Love, together with prayer and the restrictions in the food consumption, signifies a different way of existence that the faithful choose. Life becomes something which is based on love—a relationship with God and other creatures—instead of "life" grounded on the death of other beings which enables an individual survival. This is also the reason why Eucharist has always had the central place in the Christian life, representing the Church itself. In Eucharist eating and drinking, that is internalizing the very material of our hypostasis, is an act of communion, not of individuality. By *eating* Christ's body and *drinking* His blood, the faithful choose love as a relational way of existence to be their true nature and the foundation of their life.

existence in the fallen world results in the human inability to create. Seen from this perspective, the human being seems to become an icon of the ancient gods or the *Demiurge*, who can deal with matter and the world in various ways, but can never actually overcome their boundaries. Ancient Greek gods are not ontologically free beings but behave merely as super-creatures. To some extent it could be said that they represent "super-humans" of the natural state. They have extraordinary capacities that operate within this world, but are unable to overcome it.[2] This can explain why the concept of person and the idea of human creation were simultaneously absent from the ancient Greek thought, in spite of the fact that the Greeks shaped extraordinary sculptures and paintings. For an ontology in which nature, cosmos (order), or essence is the foundation of existence, ontological freedom and the capacity of creation *ex nihilo* remain alien concepts.

The relation between the existence of the human being and things in the world changes radically if we understand human beings in terms

[2] A similar comment could be made in respect to contemporary "heroes" and "stars" of popular culture. Many of the superheroes of Hollywood movies could be called "natural super-beings" even when they perform seemingly supernatural acts. This is because they represent an incarnation of the hyper-utilization of the fallen world and matter. In other words, both Greek gods and modern superheroes remain the slaves of this world, being incapable of overcoming their *createdness*. Thus, in this type of popular culture even the idea of God is subjected to the fallen ontology and its logic. God is perceived primarily as a "superman" whose function is to perform miracles (which means to make use of this world as it is, in a magic-like manner) or to make human life as comfortable as possible within the limits of this world. The idea that human beings should be liberated from the fallen state ("this world") and their own (*natural*) nature is absent. Thus, even ethics in this light becomes just a means of subordinating human beings to the fallen state, not a means for human liberation. We can notice here how the very logic of formally religious iconography and religious narratives can become profoundly non-Christian and often effectively anti-Christian. Many of the widespread religious ideas of God and religion appear to be more destructive than atheism for the Christian understanding of God-world relations.

of personhood. The human being-world relation is marked then primarily by the *free presence* of both the human being in the world and the world itself. To exist as a person, as we have seen, implies the idea of freedom from pre-determination of any sort. In Christian understanding, the human being is an open project, a being capable of overcoming the boundaries of the pre-given world. Personhood is then essentially a transcendental reality. This does not mean, however, that the human being miraculously escapes the necessity of pre-given presence and individuality. It means rather that each human being has a potential to develop his or her freedom in respect to the necessity of nature and the compelling presence of "this world."[3] This opportunity is given to human beings in the Church, i.e., in the Eucharist. However, even such overcoming of the necessities that human beings face in ecclesial hypostasis, appears in the course of history through the icon of what is to come. History is only the beginning of the process which is to be completed in the *eschaton*.

These two different understandings of what the human being is and the condition of the human relation to the world, define the way

[3]A short clarification might be needed here in relation to the usage of the construction of "this world."

"This world" primarily signifies the state of necessity due to: (1) createdness of beings, for which their own nature is a necessity; and (2) the Fall, which signifies the choice of an autonomous existence outside the relation with God as a foundation of the human existence. Thus, "this world" and liberation from it has nothing to do with a "body-soul" dualism, or "matter-spirit" antagonism, if we understand these concepts as a parallel existence of two realities (in, for example, Neo-Platonist sense). The only duality that, in my view, can be justified from an Orthodox Christian perspective is the duality between the state of necessity (corruption) and the state of freedom, not between "body" as a visible reality and "soul" as an airy, phantomlike counterpart of the human body, which is *a priori* free from the boundaries of "this world." It seems to me that this is precisely the sense in which the verses from the New Testament contrasting the "world" and the "Kingdom of God" should be understood (cf. Jn 3.6; Jn 15.19; Jn 17.6, 14, 16; 1 Cor 15.50). Only by entering the "new creation" can this world can be both rescued and justified.

we approach the problem of human creativity. We can take, on the one hand, the priority of individual ontology as the criterion for human existence in the world, which would lead to the confirmation of the human being in his/her atomized state. Accordingly, all particular beings and things in the world exist as *facts*, as necessary and compelling presences, including individual existence. This is then also true for human creative activities (e.g., artworks) that become just particles of the objectivized, individualized world in which the human presence is reduced to its createdness. On the other hand, applying the personal way of human existence and human-world relation, things in the world are not revealed as compelling *facts* but become the reality through which the human being relates with his or her freedom and love.[4]

2.2 Creation as "Event": Overcoming the Necessity of Pre-Given Matter

If we try to analyze concrete examples of modern and contemporary artworks based on the distinction we have just made, we can draw interesting conclusions regarding the necessities that human beings, following Zizioulas, face when trying to genuinely create.

If we return for a moment to Zizioulas' analysis of art, we find that in front of a painting Zizioulas is focused on human presence in absence which, in his view, is a consequence of human individuality and the fact that the human being cannot create matter itself. Instead, the human being is forced to use pre-existing matter in an attempt to create, which automatically nullifies the very attempt to create, leading to its failure.

---

[4]Making a distinction between different modalities of human relation to the world, that result in different ways of existence of things in the world for the human being, in terms of subjectivism vs objectivism would be entirely misleading in this context. The objective existence of the world is not rejected here in favor of the priority of any subjective (or arbitrary) perception, imagination, or "inner world." The distinction that I make here takes place on the level of the conflict between *being as necessity* and *existence as freedom*, two different but not unrelated realities.

Although Zizioulas does not explicitly name other artistic media, the same logic can be applied to any fine-arts category. This means that what is taken here to be at the same time a work of art and human creation is a *piece* having some form and being made of certain materials. These materials can include not only canvas, colors, and stone, but also air-vibrations in the case of music, light and photo-sensitive material in the case of photography, and even the human body itself in the case of dance or theater. This understanding of human creative works is "factual" since their basic character is sought in certain material data that can be observed and aesthetically appreciated. In this sense, artworks as "facts" are witnesses to the human (in)ability to create matter. This logic seems unavoidable if we identify creation with the production of a certain *thing*.

Instead of proposing some *meta* content of a creative act, or modernist concepts of "imagination" and "inspiration" as keys to understanding what a creative subject and creative works are, my intention is to propose an approach that understands a creative act as an *event* rather than a "piece" or a set of certain "facts." If we suppose that a creative act is a broader category that cannot be reduced to material or aesthetical data, we can seek its origin not in the material the artist uses to produce a piece or in the artist's intentions and mental processes, but in the very existential *movement* of the human being while performing a creative act. This movement leads toward crossing the boundaries of the self (one's own, pre-given presence as an individual), which is the reason why it can be called *ecstatic* in character. If we consider creation primarily in terms of this ecstatic movement of person, it seems that it is no longer necessary to look at the matter that can be used in concrete examples of human creation as an obstacle and a compelling presence that prevents human beings from creating.

In order to clarify this issue I will present several modern/contemporary art practices. I find these practices relevant and helpful in my goal to show (1) the limitations of an approach that reduces a creative attempt primarily to the "facts," and (2) possible ways for overcoming the necessities of the pre-given matter and pre-given presence in general, in a creative act. After a brief introduction describing the general features of the examples, I will focus on a more specific analysis of each in light of the issues described in the previous chapter.

* * *

The first example is the "ready-made" practice, which is primarily associated with the work of Marcel Duchamp. To produce "ready-mades" in Duchamp's case means to take average useful objects and "proclaim" them "artworks." It is usually assumed that the "Bicycle Wheel" was the first Duchamp's ready-made.[5] He took a bicycle wheel, turned it upside down fixing it to a chair. In this work, the artist used mechanically produced artifacts that have a practical value in daily life (a bicycle wheel and a chair). They are, however, taken out of their usual context to make a new, *useless* construction. One could remark that in this case the production of an artwork is still dependant on the manual work (fixing the wheel to the chair), no matter how minimal this manual labor is. Duchamp soon abandoned this practice, eliminating manual interventions completely in his mature ready-made works. This can be seen in arguably the best known ready-made—*Fountain* (Figure 1). *Fountain* is a simple urinal which is de-functionalized, dislocated from its usual context (toilet) and exhibited as a work of art in the gallery (signed *R. Mutt*). Objects such as this urinal that Duchamp exhibits as pieces of art are not made, envisioned, or shaped by the artist. The artist

---

[5]Duchamp himself characterized this work as his "first ready-made": "The Bicycle Wheel is my first ready-made, so much so that, at first, it wasn't even called a ready-made. . . . In a way, it was simply letting things go by themselves and having a sort of created atmosphere in a studio, in an apartment where you live. Probably it serves to help your ideas come out of your head." Marcel Duchamp, in Schwarz, 1969: 442; also quoted in Moffitt, 2003: 230.

only uses objects that are already there to demonstrate his *decision* to make art out of them.

An even more radical case is the example of "emptiness" and "absence" as artistic creation. These phenomena represent some of the crucial stages in the process of the disappearance of all elements we have traditionally associated with art in previous times. I will point here to three examples that demonstrate different types of emptiness and absence as art. I believe they, together with ready-mades, shed light on the problem of using pre-existing matter in creative attempts of the human being, as well as on the problem of the compelling presence of things in the world and our own existence.

The first and the most critical manifestation of emptiness as art comes with Yves Klein and his *Le Vide* exhibition in Paris at the Iris Clert gallery in 1958 (Figure 2). The artist presented an empty gallery with white-colored walls as an artistic exhibition, offering emptiness as art. A complete absence of any objects, artworks, or even artistic interventions enables us to face the "zero" point of artistic creation, the final logical consequence of the expulsion of all elements of manual production in art, above all, the reshaping of rough material which traditionally characterized art. Art as *techne*, in other words, ends in nothingness. It becomes possible to interpret *nothing* as the pre-condition of an artistic creation.[6]

The next example, Richard Long's "A Line Made by Walking" (Figure 3), shifts focus from emptiness as such, to a specific case, the absence of the artist's body. Long was walking up and down in a field, along an imaginary straight line, until he actually made a line visible in the grass, as a result of the actions of his body. If we try to point to a concrete "piece" of art, we realize that it is a meaningless task, since nothing in particular is artwork (e.g., grass, walking, artist's body

---

[6]For more on my thesis on the constant disappearance of the *techne*-elements from modern art, in favor of *creation*, see Džalto, 2010.

performing the action, and so forth). A creative act is rather a *situation* or *event* which was brought into existence by the artist's actions and by actual absence of the artist's body from the site. When one looks at the photograph with knowledge of how the line was made, the landscape becomes instantaneously transformed from just a landscape into a specific site with artistic meaning.

Andy Warhol takes another step in making the absence of the artist's body the origin of art in his *Invisible Sculpture* (Figure 4). Warhol first stood on a podium in the club "Area" in New York. Then he moved away, "creating" an "invisible sculpture." The only thing left on the site was the inscription attached to the wall, containing his name, the title of the work, medium notice ("mixed media"), and the year. The empty space, opened by removing the artist's body from the site, becomes "art." In some sense *Invisible Sculpture* is a combination of Klein's "emptiness" and Long's "absence," since Warhol's work is actually the emptiness made as the result of the absence of the artist's body.

In the context of art as "absence" we find a very radical approach to the "absence" of the artist in a late twentieth-century art project by Donald Rodney, called "Autoicon." Rodney was suffering from sickle-cell anemia, which finally caused his death in March 1998. Before he died, Rodney had envisioned an art project which should have continued to be active after his death. The project consists of an interactive website (http://www.iniva.org/autoicon/) by which the visitor can virtually "communicate" with the (dead) artist (Figure 5).

* * *

It is clear that the idea of artistic production as a unique piece shaped out of some rough material is not sufficient to grasp the meaning of the concept of creativity in these examples. Creation in these examples cannot be reduced to the human attempt to create, which fails due to the usage of the pre-existing matter.

In the following subchapters I will analyze more closely the above presented examples in order to find a solution to (1) the problem of pre-existing matter, and (2) the problem of individuality. I think that all of these examples point to freedom from pre-existing matter in the following ways: (1) by transformation of the pre-given matter from a necessary presence into a free presence (examples of ready-mades); (2) by absence of matter as a *conditio sine qua non* of the creative activities (example of emptiness); (3) by the absence of the artist's body, which becomes the source of creation (examples of the works by Long, War-hol, and Rodney). All of these examples, in my view, offer a solution to the problem of individuality as well, by pointing to the communal dimension of the creative act.

The first problem, pre-existing matter, and solutions to it will be explored in subchapters 2.2.1 to 2.2.3, while the problem of individuality and solutions to it will be analyzed in subchapter 2.3.

2.2.1 READY-MADES

Ready-mades represent one of the most provocative artistic method-ologies of the twentieth century. There are a number of aspects that can be addressed in relation to the question of creativity and ready-mades as well as their position within the modern concept of art. I will focus here only on the strategy of "choosing" objects, which in my view is central for the topic of creativity within the ready-made practice.

"Choosing" objects as a way of artistic creation was defined by Duchamp himself, in his attempt to describe his own task in ready-mades.[7] The artist uses an object which is already there, but he is the

---

[7]In 1917 Duchamp submitted his *Fountain* for an exhibition in New York. When the work was rejected Duchamp published a letter explaining his views on art. I quote only the passage relevant to his strategy of "choosing objects": "Whether Mr. Mutt with his own hands made the fountain or not has no importance. He CHOSE it. He took an ordinary article of life, placed it so that its useful significance

one who *decides* to make art out of that mundane object. This approach challenges the traditional understanding of what art and the creative processes are. We now face a question that seems absurd: is it necessary for a visual artist to physically make something in order to *create* art? Clearly the artist in this case does not participate by any means in the production of the material object. He is also not the creator of a concept according to which professional workers fabricate a concrete thing. He simply uses things that are already there and makes them "art." The next question is, why should these things be considered artwork or creation at all? Why does a urinal, which in the plumbing shop is just a urinal, become "art" when Duchamp decides it should be art? Where is the origin of the creative quality of *Fountain*?

One of the most convincing explanations of how and why *Fountain* becomes art comes from the so-called "institutional theory" of art. According to George Dickie, a certain object becomes art as a part of the "system" in which art is generated. Art appears as a complex web of institutions (galleries, museums, curators, art-dealers, artists, art historians, theoreticians, magazines, books on art, art fairs, and so forth) which is the frame in which art is being produced.[8] The artist is

disappeared under the new title and point of view—created a new thought for that object." Duchamp, 2008: 252.

[8]In many respects the "institutional theory of art" of Dickie and the "art world" theory of Arthur Danto are complementary, as they both refer to an institutional framework in which something becomes art. In contrast to Dickie, who accentuates the whole web of institutions and procedures that make the "system of art" and generate artistic value, Danto accentuates the significance of "theory" which makes a framework for an object (such as Warhol's "Brillo Boxes") to become art. "Theory" is thus a key link between a piece and the "artworld" in which the piece can function as art. George Dickie uses Danto's concept of the "artworld" in developing his "institutional theory of art." He describes it as "the broad social institution in which works of art have their place" (Dickie, 1974: 29). Dickie thus explicitly points to "the institutional essence of art" (ibid. 32), as well as to the whole range of occupations and institutions that actually constitute "artworld" as a "social institution" (see ibid. 33, 34). The basic idea we can grasp from both the "artworld" and

only one part of it, and not necessarily the most important one. He or she produces a work ("artifact") but it is up to the "system" to recognize it, appreciate it and finally adopt it into the artworld (or "institution of art") making a "work of art" out of an "artifact."[9]

This theory successfully explains how the diverse entities that we see in the history of modern and contemporary art can all be called "art," despite the fact that they have nothing in common regarding their formal elements, structure, appearance, meaning, or content. From this theory we also learn that there are no *a priori* qualities that a work of art must possess in order to qualify for "art work" status. It successfully explains the mechanism by which something becomes a part of the "class" of art, which means something exhibited, promoted, and finally accepted by many "relevant" people as art. This theory, consequently, does not consider creation as a relevant concept for the production of artworks. Therefore, although this explanation fits perfectly into the framework of understanding "art" as primarily a modern construct and function within modern (bourgeois) society, we have to return to the very decisions that the artist makes and to the *phenomenology* of his strategy if we want to see *if it is a creation* and *why*, rather than *if it is art* and *why*. This sheds new light on the act of Duchamp compared with the institutional theory of art.

In Duchamp's strategy we recognize some elements of the modern idea of artist as "genius," which is so remarkably underlined in one passage from Lessing's drama *Emilia Galotti*. It is the idea that the artist has a special "gift" or "talent" by which he almost miraculously produces art

"institutional" theory of art is that there is a broader social "system," "institutions" or a "world" in which something functions as "art." According to it, there are not any formal conditions a work must fulfill, nor any metaphysical properties it must have in order to become "art." The quality of being "art" consists in belonging to the "artworld," to what the professionals and other people participating in it accept as "art."

    [9]Cf. Dickie, 1974: 34, 38.

works, quite independently of any manual or skilled work, which Lessing addresses in the question "can there be an artist without hands?"[10] This fascination with the extraordinary capacities of "talented spirits" or "individuals" is typical of early modern times. We should not forget that it is precisely this atmosphere of the Enlightenment period in which the modern concept of art was formulated. Duchamp acts as someone who has the capacity to "bring things into being" unrelated to manual labor, material, or visual characteristics or appearance of the piece. Everything he chooses can potentially become his creation. It seems as if he operates according to the idea of the artist as *Divino Artista*,"[11] whose extraordinary capacities and skills create works that look almost as if not made by human hands. However, we immediately notice some essential distinctions: in contrast to the modern idea of "genius," Duchamp has no intention to produce any objects of *aesthetic pleasure*. He also does not demonstrate any special gift, talent, or skill compared with other people. Anyone can employ the very same method in art production. This way Duchamp's intervention subverts the idea of modern art as primarily an aesthetic-based discipline, and the modern idea of the artist as a uniquely talented individual who produces extraordinary works ("masterpieces"). He subscribes to the

[10]"Und doch bin ich wiederum sehr zufrieden mit meiner Unzufriedenheit mit mir selbst.—Ha! dass wir nicht unmittelbar mit den Augen malen! Auf dem langen Wege, aus dem Auge durch den Arm in den Pinsel, wie viel geht da verloren!—Aber, wie ich sage, dass ich es weiß, was hier verloren gegangen, und wie es verloren gegangen, und warum es verloren gehen müssen: darauf bin ich ebenso stolz, und stolzer, als ich auf alles das bin, was ich nicht verloren gehen lassen. Denn aus jenem erkenne ich, mehr als aus diesem, dass ich wirklich ein großer Maler bin; dass es aber meine Hand nur nicht immer ist.—Oder meinen Sie, Prinz, dass Raphael nicht das größte malerische Genie gewesen wäre, wenn er unglücklicherweise ohne Hände wäre geboren worden? Meinen Sie, Prinz?" Gotthold Ephraim Lessing, *Emilia Galotti* (quoted here after G. E. Lessing, 2006: *Emilia Galotti*. Cologne, Anaconda, 10–11).
[11]See Kris, Kurz, 1980: 74–86; also Badt, 1968: 85–102.

"genius" concept—he does not even need to *make* anything in order to create (which seems a literal illustration of Lessing's paradigm)—while he actually negates its exclusiveness and the naivety of the modern idea of autonomous art. In some sense his strategy points to creative capacities per se (as bringing things into being) and to the *democratization* of art. This means that creativity should be understood as a universal human capacity that can occur anywhere at any time. In this sense it can also be said that by "choosing" objects Duchamp negates art as a modern bourgeois construct, affirming *creation* as a universal human capacity.[12]

[12]This is a very subversive idea within modern society, which questions the importance of a whole set of institutions as well as the modern "story of art," making them basically irrelevant. If anyone can be a creator of art without the institution's approval, then it is impossible to control it via institutional mechanisms. This renders these institutions useless and, at the same time, prevents artistic creation from functioning primarily as another commodity within the logic of capitalist society. However, one could also present a counter argument that it is precisely within the institution that Duchamp's strategy makes sense and where it actually becomes art. Although this is true for most of Duchamp's later works, it should not be forgotten that the first ready-made was produced in a private space (the artist's studio) and that *Fountain* was also rejected from the first exhibition It was sent to (which enabled Duchamp to write his article "The Richard Mutt Case" [1917] as a kind of "ready-made" manifesto. See Duchamp, 2008). Further development of Duchamp's concepts, in my view, allows us to understand his work as a fundamental challenge to the idea of art as a "system," in which his own works become artworks. The most striking example of this aspect is playing chess, which Duchamp intensely practiced from 1923 and which became his major known activity by the end of the 1920s (see Ades, 1999: 140). *Art as a chess play* makes art "virtual," free from any objects. In this context creation can be understood as a concept that exists primarily in human minds and is developed through the mutual exchange of ideas among the players. The chess board and figures become symbols of the conceptual process. It is not by chance that the conceptual artists, whose intention was also to turn art into "ideas" and "dematerialize" it in order to liberate art from its market role and institutional existence, turned to Duchamp as their spiritual father. That way, in their view, art became "more human," something which is in the most basic way connected to the human being. (For more on this topic see Džalto, 2007: 35–49.)

But what is really *creative* in the ready-made strategy? Is it not an attempt to negate the very concept of creativity in art production? If we try to define creativity in this case merely as an innovative approach within a particular historical period, do we return then to the modern idea of originality? If we bear in mind the concept of artistic creation as it is usually understood in respect to art works of the past it can certainly be interpreted that way. However, I see another possibility. To see Duchamp's strategy as a creation one must reject the concept of creation as making something original by shaping material in a new and unexpected manner. Creativity appears as bringing things not into factual (objectivized) existence, but as bringing them into a personal relation in which they become a part of a personal presence. This point can be illustrated by an Old Testament story.

In the beginning of the book of Genesis we find a method of creation quite similar to Duchamp's creation in the ready-made works. In the second chapter of Genesis, God brings animals to Adam to "see what he would name them; whatever the man called each of them would be its name" (Gen 2.19). As the story goes, "the man gave names to all the cattle, and the birds of the air, and all the wild animals" (Gen 2.20). To understand this point we have to recall the significance and mean-ing of names in biblical terminology. A *name* signifies the character of someone or something holding the specific name, but also its essence.[13] Consequently, to give a name to someone or something, or to re-name them, means that someone or something is given life or enters a new life from the moment the name is given. It is significant that the very character of names implies a relation between the giver of the name and its holder. This is the reason why in the biblical tradition to name someone or something does not simply imply a fact of recognition of

[13]Cf. ODJR, 492–493. E. A. Speiser interprets the function of names in a similar way: "Names were regarded not only as labels but also as symbols, magical keys as it were to the nature and essence of the given being or thing." Speiser, in AB:16.

their existence, but a special personal relation in which this existence is being constituted.[14] We thus realize that Adam in this story acts in fact as a second "creator." Although God created everything, including animals, Adam appears as the re-creator of the creation, a friend of God who participates in God's creative acts.[15] Adam is not able to bring matter into existence but he creates by transforming the already given things (animals in this case) from a necessary presence into a personal free presence. The way he performs this act is similar to God's creation. God creates everything by speaking, calling everything by name from non-being into being, as Adam also calls beings by name from a

[14]The topic of the significance and function of names in the Bible is a very complex one and expands far beyond the purposes of this work. To support the above interpretations I will point here to a couple of examples of the context in which the the term "name" appears, as well as examples of the act of "giving name(s)" in the Bible. The ability to bestow a name is a privilege and signifies authority (cf. Gen 2.18), but giving names is also a sign of a specific function or a relationship (Gen 35.17–18). A name can indicate the character of the person bearing it, and names were often given as a result of some circumstance at birth or later in life (Gen 10.25, 19.22, 25.30, but also Gen 25.26). Giving a name to another person is a sign of a close relationship and unity (Is 4.1, Deut 28.9–10). Contrary to giving names stands the idea of "destroying," "taking away" or "forgetting" someone's name (cf. Jer 23.27) as the total negation of a personal identity and even a person's existence. Based on these examples it can be said that the name implies a personal identity, presence, and existence. It is not only a verbal symbol attached to someone/something but with no essential connection to the person or thing. Names in the Bible stand for the beings they are attached to, signifying their identity. The extraordinary significance of names can also be seen in the following examples: God's name should not be said (Ex 20.6); those who will live in the future Kingdom of God (eternal life) have their names "written in the book of life" (Rev 20.15, 21.27); baptism of those joining the Church is performed "in the name of the Father, and of the Son, and of the Holy Spirit" (Mt 28.19). Cf. also "Name, Namengebung" in LTK, Vol. VII, 624–629. Related to the problem of God's name see also a recent study by Rodoljub Kubat: "יהוה—The Making-Himself-Present-God of the Old Testament" (Kubat, 2007).

[15]Cf. to the "Akt des Nachschaffens" and the accompanying explanations of the verse from Genesis in Claus Westermann's *Genesis*, Westermann, 1976: 310–312.

non-personal objectivized existence into a personal relation. The name of these creatures signifies their existence in a personal relation with Adam as the "king" of God's creation. The creatures are thus not faceless objects anymore, but living beings that Adam *knows by name*.[16]

Duchamp does something similar, regardless of whether or not he intended a reference to this biblical story. He takes objects that are already there and "calls" ("names") them "art." The artist's choice makes this object a creation. The choice as a means of creation implies two further things: (1) choosing an object, to become a work of art, the object becomes specific, distinct from all other objects; (2) the specific character and identity of a ready-made object is the result of the personal presence of the artist in his act of choosing.[17] An ordinary object that

---

[16]The concept of "knowledge" has significantly different connotations in a Christian perspective compared to the common understanding of this concept. God does not "know" the world *objectively* (neutrally), the knower and the object of knowledge are not "two opposite partners," in Zizioulas' words (see Zizioulas, 1985: 102–104). God *knows* the world through His love, He *sees* (we could also say *contemplates* and also *judges*) the world in Christ. God "remembers," "knows," and "forgets" through Christ and Christ's communion with the world. Everything that enters a relationship with God (in and through Christ) exists. On the contrary, everything that has no relation with God, he "forgets," which means that all that has no *real* existence. The communal dimension of knowledge is underlined in the very biblical text too, where "knowing" becomes a concept which describes even the sexual intercourse between man and woman as an act of communion (cf. Gen 4.1, 4.17, 4.25).

[17]We can also say that "choosing" objects or "naming" beings signifies their entrance into a personal relation, from the state of necessity, individuality, and alienation. A telling story from a literary context can best illustrate this difference in the mode of existence. It is a story from *The Little Prince* by Antoine de Saint-Exupéry, in which the fox explains to the Prince the difference between his rose and many other beautiful roses (to this example Zizioulas also refers as an illustration of the "ontology of love," see Zizioulas, 1985: 49, fn. 43):

" 'Go and look again at the roses. You will understand now that yours is unique in all the world.' . . . The little prince went away, to look again at the roses. 'You are not at all like my rose,' he said. 'As yet you are nothing. No one has tamed you, and

is transformed into art signifies a personal dimension of its existence as a creation. In other words, it is not any particular formal quality that causes a simple object to become a free creation, but the presence of a person, to whom an object is brought into a relation.[18] In that sense, moving objects from the state of being merely things into a personal presence marks the creative moment. Creation thus does not consist in re-shaping pre-given matter, but in giving it a new way of being; a new existence in a personal relation.

There are, however, other perspectives related to Duchamp's creative act as demonstrated in ready-mades. I mentioned the institutional theory as an alternate view according to which the transformation from merely an object into an artwork takes place within the institution or the system of art. At this point I would say that it is true that the change from a non-art thing into an artwork takes place within the system of art, which serves primarily social, ideological, and market purposes. However, the question of art as an institution should be sharply distinguished from the question of creation. Ready-mades are particularly interesting in regard to this question. It has usually been thought

you have tamed no one. You are like my fox when I first knew him. He was only a fox like a hundred thousand other foxes. But I have made him my friend, and now he is unique in all the world.' . . . 'You are beautiful, but you are empty,' he went on. 'One could not die for you. To be sure, an ordinary passerby would think that my rose looked just like you—the rose that belongs to me. But in herself alone she is more important than all the hundreds of you other roses . . . Because she is *my* rose." (Antoine de Saint-Exupéry, *The Little Prince*, chapter XXI)

[18]Similar approach can also be seen in Minimal art. "Average objects" or "merely things" are used as art signifying a personal presence of the artist (who made them "art") by means of the artist's absence. This absence is underlined in the minimal works as they are, in many instances (e.g., Carl Andre and Robert Morris), intentionally *fabricated* (not made by artist) or *chosen* (out of the already existing things) with no physical or visual traces of the artist's personality or any activities (as brush strokes, imprints or carvings, for instance). In these examples, we are faced with an *underlined* absence that stresses the artist's presence in absence. (Cf. Džalto, 2007: 51–64)

that the de-functionalizing of useful objects, in order for them to be newly contextualized, is the essential aspect of Duchamp's practice. Apart from the importance of this strategy for questioning the social and institutional function of art, Duchamp comes close to another important issue that implies the concept of person in his works. By liberating objects from their utility Duchamp presents them as objects with no purpose whatsoever. This purposelessness forces us to rethink the system or institution of art, since it is precisely in this institutional context that artworks become useful again, specifically for social, ideological, and market purposes. In addition, it forces us to consider the purposelessness of art as an aesthetic ideal in modern times. This recalls Kant's definition of aesthetic pleasure and beauty, as well as the nineteenth-century idea of *l'art pour l'art*.[19] The point of Duchamp's purposelessness is that the very purposelessness is not independent from the human being, regardless of how paradoxical this may seem. In fact, this purposelessness of artworks, as well as their existence, comes out of the interactions between the persons involved in the creative activity. This also suggests that purposeless, one could even say *absurd*, objects appear as an icon of the very basic properties of personhood. We should remember that being a person also has no other purpose apart from one's very existence as a person.[20] Can it be said that purposeless things that exist as a result of human creative activity are nothing more than an icon of their originator, the human person, and of the purposelessness of the personal existence, when this existence is

---

[19]These ideas seem to oppose understanding art as a system or social institution. However, they actually appear as very useful ideas within the system of art. Aesthetic "neutrality" and "innocence" of art were, from the very beginning of the modern idea of art, an appropriate cover for the social functioning of art. A good example of this is the political and ideological dimension to the formation of the Louvre museum during the French Revolution (more closely analyzed in chapter IV).

[20]Cf. Zizioulas' words: "the goal is the person itself." Zizioulas, 1985: 47.

achieved? In this sense, paradoxically, purposeless things point to the person and to creation as a singular human capacity, as "purposiveness without purpose" (Kant).[21]

Does it mean, then, that this creation is completely free from the necessity of pre-given things, if the artist still uses material pre-given objects in his art? This question, in my view, can be answered affirmatively: such a creation can be free from pre-given matter even though the artist uses pre-given objects to create. In spite of the fact that objects, as parts of the material reality that exists independently from the artist, are used in the artistic creation, the creation does not consist in the formal/physical qualities of the objects. Duchamp manages to liberate his creation from matter as a compelling presence. Creation comes out of a *personal presence* and it is this presence that the objects began to signify since they entered their new existence through this *personal relation*. The artist in this example re-creates in a similar way to Adam's; he causes transformation of the objects as "facts" into a free personal presence.[22] In that sense, the one and the same object both is and is not the same: as merely an object, the urinal remains what it is—a material, individualized, and distant object. On the other hand, a urinal becomes distinct from all other urinals when it is "chosen" from the rest of the objects, thereby obtaining a special significance. Objects then function as *a means* of demonstrating the creative act, but they also become

[21]See Kant, 1977: 143.

[22]Verena Krieger, for instance, characterizes Duchamp's creation as a "spiritual act" in contrast to material production, although without any intention of ascribing to it a theological argument: "Die künstlerische Schöpfung ist damit kein materieller Schöpfungsakt mehr, sondern ein rein geistiger Vorgang. . . . Denn während der Künstler als 'alter deus'—analog dazu, wie Gottvater Adam aus Lehm gebildet und ihm anschließend den Atem eingehaucht hat—ein Bildwerk schuf und es lebendig erscheinen ließ, macht Marcel Duchamp sich selbst die Hände nicht mehr schmutzig. Kunstschaffen ist ein rein philosophischer Akt geworden; die Kunst wirkt nicht primär auf den Gesichtssinn, sondern auf das Reflexionsvermögen." Krieger, 2007: 152.

transformed via the same creative act, from the state of necessity into a free presence.

2.2.2 "VOID"

The example of "void" work offers a different perspective. Unlike ready-made in which we still deal with objects, the "material" that the artist uses in this case is *emptiness*. This is the crucial moment in the process of liberation of the artist from manual labor and pre-given presences. It seems that in order to be able to create freely, the artist had to come to "nothing" which alone could guarantee a free and genuine act of creation. This reductionism can be seen as the end of art as a *techne*-based discipline. Art as *techne* (τέχνη) implies the usage of pre-given matter that is shaped through the manual, skilled activity of the *tech-nites* (artist). However, in the visual arts *techne* also implies mimesis as well as a certain concept of beauty. These basic elements that constitute the meaning of the *techne* concept survived ancient culture and were employed again in the eighteenth century in formulating the new idea of fine arts (*beaux arts*). At the same time art begins to signify creation, inspiration, and originality, together with the *techne* elements inherited from earlier times. Art became a new social function within the newly born bourgeois society. This amalgam of various, sometimes mutually incompatible concepts, together with the idea that fine arts should be an autonomous discipline, is what primarily caused the transformation of the *techne* elements, a transformatio that led art, in the end, to the "void."[23] It could be said that *art as techne* dies to enable *art as creation*. This process led creative tendencies in art to negate the presence of any pre-given matter or any necessity the artist deals with, in favor of free creation. This should not be surprising given the connection we

[23]This conceptual inconsistency which became the immanent property of the new idea of "art" I elsewhere called "the inner conflict" of the modern idea of art. See Džalto, 2010.

have established between freedom and creativity. It seems that freedom is affirmed at the cost of all formal, visual, and material elements in the creative process, as only *nothingness* could secure freedom and creation.[24]

It is important to bear in mind the explicit reference which Klein made with his "void" exhibition to Eastern spirituality and, more particularly, Zen Buddhism. David Hopkins points to this connection very clearly as Klein's quest for a "liberating immateriality": "Klein thus conceived himself as the prophet of a liberating 'immateriality'. His *Le Vide* . . . obviously embodied the notion of a spiritually energized emptiness. (Zen Buddhism, which he became aware of on a trip to Japan in 1952–53, similarly embraces 'nothingness' . . .)."[25] In contrast to Duchamp who enables objects to pass from the state of necessity into a free presence, the "void" stresses the "nothing" out of which creation should appear.

Here one can ask a question similar to that in Duchamp's case: In what way does emptiness enable creation? It seems that creation here is understood primarily in negative terms. Emptiness and nothingness come as a result of the liberation of the creative field from using pre-given matter, but it is still not clear what would be the content of such a creation. If we understand freedom as freedom "from" and freedom "for" at the same time, we should identify what this freedom affirms, what is its positive content that is grasped through the affirmation of freedom and liberation from necessity?

There is no doubt that Klein sought an aesthetic quality of the void, together with a different understanding of special and all other

---

[24]At this point it becomes possible to speak of the theological significance of the very process of art history. It becomes a history of the liberation of creativity from the essence- and individuality-based ontology represented by *techne*. From this perspective it could be said, somewhat provocatively, that the existence of creation directly depends on the death of art both as a social function and as *techne*. Further implications of this topic are developed in the concluding chapter.

[25]Hopkins, 2000: 79.

perceptual qualities of emptiness. However, Klein himself was pointing to the human content of this emptiness, something that has to do
with human presence in absence. In his "Chelsea Hotel Manifesto" Klein
states: " . . . the void has always been my constant preoccupation; and I
hold that in the heart of the void as well as in the heart of man, fires are
burning."[26] The human content as a fundamental property of this void
seems to be underlined with the text to the exhibition's opening invita-
tion: "Iris Clert invites you to honor, with all of your affective presence,
the lucid and positive advent of a certain reign of the sensible. The per-
ceptive synthesis of this manifestation sanctions in Yves Klein the picto-
rial quest for an ecstatic and immediately communicable emotion."[27]

The empty gallery that confronts us with its emptiness makes it clear
that we also meet concrete human beings who occupy the empty space
of the gallery, instead of only consuming some artistic or aesthetic content presented to us. The content of a creative act can then be found not
in the aesthetic properties of emptiness per se, but in the personal presences that the emptiness underlines. The void signifies a field liberated
from the necessary presences, which, at the same time, affirms the personal presences of those participating in such a "work of art" by walking
through the gallery, meeting other people, and sharing their thoughts.
The first remarkable consequence of this is that the modernist construct
of the artist as "genius" virtually disappears from creation, opening emptiness as an unconditional space of freedom in which everyone becomes
creator by the power of his or her personal presence.[28] This way, the
whole paradigm of creativity and ingeniousness as exclusive properties
of particular individuals can be read as having an iconic character (if
we set aside for a moment the social and ideological implications of
"genius" and other related concepts). Creative capacities and ingenious-

[26]Yves Klein, quoted after Restany, 2005: XV.

[27]Restany, 2005: 11.

[28]This aspect became one of the central points of reference in the early manifestations of performance and happening, in which Klein participated as well.

ness appear as the very properties of personhood—i.e., the properties of each human being that participate in the image of God. Another conclusion we can reach is that creative capacities, as a property of each human being, do not require any artistic content or any institutional framework in order to appear. If we again try to read the history of modern art as having an iconic character, we can at this point note that the very idea of art, not only genius or other particular concepts related to it (e.g., talent or inspiration), can be read as having an iconic character. They become a metaphor of creativity as a universal human capacity, which is related to the uniqueness of each human person.

Therefore, everyone who wants to participate in the creation of a "work" can join; there is no fundamental difference between the artist, who is supposed to create a work of art, and the audience that is supposed to consume the artistic creation. This traditional view should not be applied to creation as emptiness because all that the artist does is simply open an empty room (both literally and metaphorically) where human beings can meet. They give a positive content to the emptiness by their actions and thoughts. This is the reason why all of those participating in this action actually become creators; they create the meaning of this "work" and the "work" itself via their presence and actions instead of simply consuming what has been placed in front of them. This is important to note, in regard to the basic capacities of the human person we acknowledged earlier, that this creation appears on the one hand as creation out of nothing (without the use of any matter for the production of a work) while, on the other hand, the creation comes out of the interpersonal relations that are established in this emptiness.

The product of this creative act is not any particular work of art but a concrete human person. This contrast between the necessity of the world and human creative activity, which requires freedom as an "abyss," is emphatically stressed by Nikolai Berdyaev. Berdyaev's understanding of freedom, which I find applicable to some extent to the issue as it appears here, underlines one central idea: freedom cannot be derived out of something pre-given (determined).[29] Therefore, freedom is based on some kind of "nothing."[30] This "nothing" should, again, be understood not as a nihilistic opposition to the world but as a positive *abyss of freedom* that enables creation to appear.[31] This "nothing" is required precisely because it does not impose any constraints on the human spirit. In this sense, we could say that both God and the human being require "nothing" (understood as freedom) to create in a genuine way. As I pointed out earlier, God's creative acts are unconditional as his freedom is equal to his existence. On the other hand, human creation out of nothing becomes the way by which human beings overcome the necessity of the world.

2.2.3 "ABSENCE"

"Emptiness" and "absence" appear as two related topics within the history of twentieth-century art. I address absence primarily in terms of the physical absence of the artist from the artwork. Absence in the case of Richard Long's "Line" is manifested as traces of his previous actions performed on the site. Looking at the photograph of the site we become aware of the artist's body by the act of the physical activity of his walking. This awareness is unavoidable since the artist's previous presence is what causes its transformation from just a landscape into a specific site. We can ask again: what should be considered creation in this case? Why should this action be considered creative at all?

[29]This is the central aspect of Berdyaev's doctrine of "*Ungrund*," which focuses on the freedom of God. However, Berdyaev applies the idea of "freedom with no origin" to the human being as well.

[30]"Our substantial nature could not be the ground for freedom. . . . Freedom is rooted in 'nothing.' The act of freedom is primordial and is completely irrational." Berdyaev, 1998: 88.

[31]"The secret of creativity is the secret of freedom. The secret of freedom is—endless and inexpressible, it is—an abyss." Berdyaev, 1996-a, Vol. I: 119.

It is clear that the work does not consist of the photograph, since it has no value as an aesthetic object but only as a medium that records a land-art project. The work, furthermore, does not consist in the artist's actions either, which would be the case if it were a performance. Finally, the landscape alone cannot be considered as a work in its formal and aesthetic qualities, independent from our awareness of its changed appearance, which is the result of the artist's actions.

The origin of the work and its creation should thus be sought in the artist's *absence*. The artist's former presence is marked by the traces he left on the site as the result of his previous activities, as a document of the previous presence of his body. The fact that the artist is not there anymore, but is nevertheless present in his absence, is what constitutes the creative act. The absence, in a manner similar to the void, becomes the "nothing" out of which creation appears.

This phenomenon is even more obvious in the example of Warhol's *Invisible Sculpture.* In some sense, it represents a combination of Long's and Klein's approach. The void is also at stake here, manifested as an absence made by the former presence of the artist. To look upon this work as a performance in its traditional sense would again be mis-leading. Creation does not consist in the artist's body or his actions, which is crucial for the phenomenology of the performance. Signifi-cantly, Warhol does not use any material or objects in order to create the art. His actual "labor" is even smaller compared to Long's, whose work still required actions that made changes to his surroundings that pointed to his absence. It is Warhol's physical *absence* from the work that becomes the origin of its creation, without any further actions. There would be no work with the artist present. His act of creation is tied to the act of making the *absence* by the removal of his physi-cal presence from the site. All other visual/material facts, such as the title or the indication of the technique, serve only to inform us of his *absent body*, which is the real "place" out of which the artist creates. It is illuminating at this point to make a comparison with Zizioulas' argument regarding human creativity. One might observe that the physical and factual absence of the artist in these examples is not a repercussion of the creative act but the other way around. One can thus reverse Zizioulas' argument, asserting that the creation in these examples appears out of the absence. Consequently, the very absence cannot be explained as the *sine qua non* consequence of the person's intention to create within the limits of the pre-given matter, as it can easily be observed that the matter in which the creative act is performed either does not exist or is virtually irrelevant. In this example it is not only the material that disappears as a necessary condition of the creation, but the artist disappears as well in order to make an empty space out of which the creative act can appear.

Warhol's work implies another important point. In front of his work one must think of the artist as a "star," which is a modified, twentieth-century interpretation of the earlier "genius" concept. The artist appears here as an extraordinary person, not primarily because of the "spiritual" qualities or skills he possesses but because of the role he plays within society and his presence in the media and public life. The case of Warhol is particularly interesting, as he was a real star of the art world, a highly visible public figure and a regular visitor of important cultural and social events. His mere appearance was enough to cause an average, every-day situation or site become *artistically* significant. The star of the art world can himself give an artistic meaning to a non-art situation or place. In such a situation, Warhol's "intervention" in a club bears artistic connotations that cause a physical place where he stood to change its meaning and significance in the absence of the signifying body. Bearing this in mind, one can also speak of a cynical aspect of the *Invisible Sculpture*. In this example the new meaning of the place originates out of the artist's disappearance not simply out of his presence as a star of the art world.

With Donald Rodney we reach the climax of the artist's absence as the source of creation. Instead of a metaphorical death of the artist in the work, death enters the work literally, making us face brutal facts of human existence. Yet, Rodney raises the issue of biological death as an artistic creation. What we see here is not only a simple absence or void as space liberated from the use of pre-given matter. Instead, the absence of the creator becomes literal, being most directly connected to the personal existence of the artist. Although morbid in some aspects, this project is a document of both the semantic and physical disappearance of the artist. He disappears from life to enter art. A *biological hypostasis*, one could postulate, is being exchanged for an *aesthetic existence*. The project is also a document of "virtualization" of the body, where the personal presence of the artist is simulated to produce artistic meaning "out of nothing," in the absence of the artist's biological existence.

Rodney's project can be understood as the final liberation of any pre-given presence in creation, including the physical, biological presence of the artist. It seems to be the final stage in the liberation of art from "necessary presences": after eliminating the material and manual execution of artwork, every pre-given presence, including the biological presence of the artist, is also removed. Artistic creation becomes possible via posthumous "communication" between the dead artist and his audience.

* * *

In the previous discussion I approached the issue of creativity from a point of view in which matter and the concept of "manufacture" in the field of visual arts are not the *sine qua non* for human creation. In respect to ready-mades, creation was explained as a personal faculty of the artist based on the artist's "decision" to make art, not on skill, talent, or the aesthetic qualities of the work. The same example clarified two further points: (1) creation can be understood as a transformation of the compelling presence of things in the world into a free personal presence; (2) creation appears as an interpersonal event, as a concept to be shared and developed by other persons.

The example of void showed a complete reduction of all material aspects of the work. The void itself becomes creation. In the works by Richard Long, Andy Warhol, and Donald Rodney creation is also liberated from the constraints of technique, matter, and skill. In these examples, the "absence" and biological death of the artist become the source out of which creation appears. The void and absence as modalities of escaping the necessity of the pre-given matter are, in one important aspect, different from God's *ex nihilo* creation. God creates not out of nothing as emptiness or void space in which creation then appears. On the contrary, he creates both space, with all the particular beings inhabiting it, and time.[32] In this respect even the emptiness of the space (e.g., the lack of any particles of matter) is still a creature, a pre-given thing, which serves as a background for the event of absence. Therefore, it is not matter itself that represents the major difficulty in an attempt to understand human creation as a demonstration of the ontological freedom, but human existence within the pre-given space-time structure as a whole. This means that any physical emptiness, even a vacuum, is also a creature, being still a part of the same space-time structure that is *created*. Thus even when the room is opened for emptiness or absence, as in the examples discussed above, this emptiness and absence is still located in the spatial-temporal structure of a creature, which is itself a necessity.

One possible way to solve this issue, which is only a specific case of the pre-giveness, is to avoid considering creation as consisting of the

[32]This is the reason why one must reject the idea of "withdrawing" as a way in which the primordial *nihil* appears, as a necessary condition of God's creation. In this respect one must agree with A. J. Torrance's critique of Moltmann's ideas of God's creation as the "withdrawing of God's presence" as the *nihil* in which the creation takes place. See Torrance, 2004: 88–91.

empty room that is left as a void, the background of the absence. As I have argued above, in the case of the void, creation should be sought in the *possibility of establishing interpersonal relations*. On the other hand, in the case of absence, creation should be sought in the *presence in absence*, which cannot be reduced to its space-time dimension. Questioning the limitations of the space-time structure of the physical emptiness is most radical in Donald Rodney's work. His biological death produces a radical absence, in that he is absent even from space-time. This highlights the importance of my main argument regarding the human presence-absence phenomenon, which is essential for understanding human capacity to create in a genuine way. Only transcendence of this space-time necessity makes human beings capable of creation out of nothing, a creation free from the boundaries of the pre-given world.

What one could also learn from these examples is that the quest for freedom from pre-given matter and pre-given presence in general can occur in a few instances: (1) by choosing objects with no personal meaning that then become a part of a personal presence; (2) by entering the void; and (3) by the absence of the artist, including the artist's biological death, which makes creation possible through human presence in absence.

My analysis has also attempted to show how the concept of creativity can be liberated from its dependence on art as a social institution, and how we can even contrast them. This makes it clear that creativity is not related primarily or only to art as a particular human activity or a social function.

In the following chapter I return to the problem of the individual as the second basic necessity, which in Zizioulas' argument prevents human beings from the full realization of their creative capacities. It might seem that the remarks made thus far do not offer any solutions to the question of whether overcoming the individuality resulting from the Fall is possible via a creative act. Can human beings be rescued from individuality with their creative capacities?

As we have seen, Zizioulas' solution to the problem of individuality can be found in the "ecclesial hypostasis," that is in overcoming an individual existence via communion with other persons and God in the Church. My goal in the following analysis is to show that human beings, too, perform an ecstatic act in the act of creation, which alone is the crucial element of personhood. By performing an ecstatic act in the most profound meaning of the word, human beings transcend their individuality.

2.3 The Creative Act as Ekstasis: Overcoming Individuality

In this chapter I address the question of whether or not individuality can be overcome by a creative act. My intention is to try to indicate the ecclesial dimension of human creative activity by exploring its ecstatic features and communal aspects implied by the very concept of *ekstasis*.

By pointing to concrete examples from artistic practice, I tried to illustrate my thesis that presence of matter does not necessarily negate genuine creation. I also suggested that the origin of creation could be sought in the presence of the person, even in the factual physical absence. What does it mean to say that the origin of creation lies in a personal presence, even if this presence is manifested as absence?

Even if we link creation with the presence of human beings, the fact remains that human beings in history are never present in a true and complete way, even if they are physically present in the here-and-now. If creation is grounded on an individual presence, it is not actually grounded on anything firm, and it again appears as an ontological impossibility. It remains an unfortunate human attempt which confirms that *creatura non potest creare*.[33] It is necessary to examine a creative act

---

[33]The creature cannot create.

more closely in order to see in what way the human being demonstrates his or her presence in history. It is also necessary to examine how a creative act can lead to overcoming presence as an ontological necessity, and the necessary absence manifested in a permanent disintegration and final disappearance (death).

My claim is that in all of the examples from artistic practice analyzed above one can find an ecstatic movement resulting in a communal dimension. This communal dimension is underlined by the participation of other human beings in the creative process. This participation of other persons (the audience or public in traditional terminology) is a constituent aspect of the work. For Duchamp a work is primarily a concept that has to be shared with other persons in order to exist and to be further developed.[34] This is why the early practice of ready-mades led Duchamp to play chess as a paradigmatic form of artistic creation.[35] Playing chess is, at the same time, always an "invention of new concepts"[36] and

[34]Verena Krieger comments in this respect that, "Duchamp betonte, der Künstler sei, 'nicht der einzige, der den Schöpfungsakt vollzieht, denn der Betrachter stellt den Kontakt des Werks mit der Umwelt her, indem er seine tieferen Eigenschaften entziffert und deutet und dadurch seinen Beitrag zum schöpferischen Prozess liefeit'. Ei veitiat die, 'Theorie . . . dass ein Kunstwerk erst existiert, wenn der Betrachter es angeschaut hat." Krieger, 2007: 153, 154.

[35]Ades, 1999: 140. For more on the importance of chess in the work of Marcel Duchamp, especially in its community dimension, see Seigel, 1997 (in particular pp. 16–26, 208–213).

[36]Cf. Dalia Judovitz's synthetic comment: "The ready-mades redefine the notion of artistic creativity, since they do not involve the manual production of objects but their intellectual reproduction." Judovitz, 1995: 76. The understanding of art as primarily a mental process and an inter-action between human beings connects Duchamp's investigations and Conceptual artists in the most profound way. Joseph Kosuth thus claims that "all art (after Duchamp) is conceptual (in nature) because art only exists conceptually" Kosuth, 1991: 18. Because of this it is capable of avoiding the market traps (in Lucy Lippard's and John Chandler's famous words: "Since dealers cannot sell art-as-idea, economic materialism is denied along with physical materialism." Lippard, Chandler: 1968: 34) being "autonomous" but it also becomes a medium of an interpersonal relation, being made "for humans" and

a communal activity, requiring an *other*: one "creator" cannot *create* in a chess play.[37]

The significance of the interpersonal dimension in the "event of art" is also crucial in Yves Klein's void. "Emptiness" as a negative definition of freedom becomes filled with creation as an interpersonal relation and human presence. This way we come to the positive content of both freedom and creation. In the "emptiness" of Klein's project, creation should be sought in the interactions of the people visiting the exhibition of nothing. The entire content of the artistic creation becomes an open space in which people meet. This example clearly shows a complete change in the traditional understanding of the artist-audience relation. In this case the artist is the one who produces *nothing* and the audience, by interpersonal relations they establish while meeting each other in the empty space, performs a creative act. The artist, in other words, becomes only one among those who create their interpersonal relations as a genuine creation, relaxed from any a priori matter, content, and form.

Since there is *nothing* that human beings confront, this emptiness becomes transformed into a personal presence via the whole web of relations the visitors establish in the empty space. *Nothing* is liberating in the sense that it does not require any pre-given presence to enable an artistic creation. *Nothing* is also challenging as it calls the visitors to

annihilating the distance between the artwork, artist and audience: "The audience of conceptual art is composed primarily of artists—which is to say that an audience separate from the participants doesn't exist" Joseph Kosuth, "Introductory Note to Art-Language by the American Editor," in Kosuth, 1991: 39. He is even more explicit in the text "Within the Context: Modernism and Critical Practice": "Where is our work? Wherever we find ourselves. Meaning is made by humans, for humans, and it is this 'making of meaning' which connects us in a real way to each other and to the world" Kosuth, 1991: 160.

[37]The ancient Latin sentence, which quite accurately describes the ecclesial dimensions of Christianity, could be paraphrased in this context reading *one artist—no artist*.

transform this radical otherness from an empty space into the field of a personal presence. This begins by the transformation of the visitors/ observers into participants/creators of the event.[38]

We can look at the "void" from another perspective as well. Klein's work can be interpreted as making the art gallery, the traditional space for art, emptied of any artistic content, such as paintings or sculptures. "Art" disappears here, as particular knowledge, skill, talent, or a modern social function. The gallery, as a substitute for the whole system of art, the place where art traditionally takes place, becomes abandoned by turning it into emptiness with no meaning per se. If there is no artwork to be brought into the gallery, exhibited, looked at and, finally, sold, a particular institution of art loses its meaning. Instead of the gallery exhibiting artworks, the empty space is filled now with living persons and "human content." Creation as a production of artifacts disappears to make room for creation as an *event*, produced by living human beings who talk, move, think, or simply shake hands in the *emptiness*.

Instead of being "extraordinary individuals," the creators discover the uniqueness of the personal identity of each human person. In this sense, the very personal identity of the human being becomes related to human creative capacities, not any particular talents or techniques.[39]

[38]The situation here is somewhat similar to the phenomenon which Robert Morris stresses in his minimalist works, by pointing to "gestalt" as their primary quality. The context and the *gestalt* of his objects highlight the importance of the "human content" which becomes more intense when facing self-referential things. In Kenneth Baker's words: "'human content' (is transferred) where it belonged, in relationships established by viewer's actions, rather then in the object." Baker, 1998: 67.

[39]Looking from a wider perspective it could be said that the conclusions made here are valid for each creation, even for those that have been made only to be "looked at," without the possibility of being formally modified or expanded by other people as in the traditional forms of art. But even in this case, the work bears this communal dimension and becomes a medium which opens itself toward us.

The "absence" works can be read in a similar fashion. They open up an empty space that becomes not simply a void but an absence as the result of the artist's former presence which marks this emptiness as a *presence in absence*. How can this particular presence in absence contribute to the topic of overcoming individuality via the creative act? We should look again for a communal dimension that could enable an escape from the isolation of individual existence. If we start from this absence as the "place" out of which a creative act appears, we will see that this absence points, almost self-evidently, to a personal presence. This presence in absence, which occurs due to the person's previous presence, is only possible if there is someone for whom this absence signifies a personal presence. In this sense a comparison to a famous example by Sartre (which Zizioulas often refers to) is instructive. In *Being and Nothingness* Sartre describes a situation in which he goes to a café expecting to meet his friend, as previously agreed. Entering the café he finds out that his friend is not there.[40] Although his friend is not physically there, he is also not entirely absent. On the contrary, the presence of his friend in his factual absence becomes a more intense presence for the author than the actual physical presence of the other people and things in the café. This "empty place" opens up by the *absence* of someone who is supposed to be there, has no meaning whatsoever for anyone else except for the one in a personal relation with the absent person. The presence of the absent person becomes more "real" than the presence of those who are outside this personal relation. This is possible not because of some emotional or psychological effect but precisely because of the character of the personal presence, which I explained earlier with the example of Adam and his "re-creation" of the world. Objective data

It is always more than what is consciously buried there. If we establish a relation to it, and via the work with the artist who painted it or other people interested in it, the work becomes a living thing. We can modify then its content, develop our own contents, further creating based on it, etc.

[40]Sartre, 1993: 9–11.

has no *a priori* meaning for a personal relation and a personal way of existence. The compelling character of the pre-given data is abandoned in a personal existence.[41]

Presence in absence thus makes sense only if there is someone to relate to this presence, manifested as absence. This is one aspect of the communal dimension of the absence works. Absence becomes the nothing out of which a creative act appears. It is absence that becomes the real "material" of the creative effort, together with the inter-personal relation between the viewer and the absent artist. This relation exists on a certain level even if we have never had the opportunity to actually meet the absent person. We are still able to relate to the absent person, having heard about him/her, having seen his/her photographs, interviews, movies, and so forth. All these do not simply provide information about the person, but bring us into a certain relation with the *energies* of the absent person. Via these *energies* this person does not exist as information or an abstract entity but as an unique personal identity.

The disappearance in the case of Donald Rodney is even more telling in this respect. The artist biologically dies but he continues to live and create at the same time through communication with other human beings. The fact that it is a computer program on the other side of the screen that really communicates with us does not affect his basic presence in absence for us. The artist also becomes present in this example through his energies that enter a relation with us. Only through this relation does the work itself become possible.

Earlier in the text I insisted on the distinction between "event" and "fact" as two different relations toward the world that might also describe the nature of a creative act in contrast to manufacturing. If we

---

[41] A radical example of the same logic we find in Hermann Hesse's *Steppenwolf*, when he puts the following words in the mouth of Hermine: "It was life and reality that were wrong."

look at the above given examples in this light, we will see that the very concept of *event* implies participation of human beings and not a single act of the "genius." This means that an event always points to a communal dimension; it implies involvement of more than one person. The point here is not in the message that is being transmitted via creation, but in the very act of a personal relation and a joint interaction which is being established.

This leads us to another aspect of the "absence" works, which makes them relevant for both the tradition of modern art and the problem of individuality. The famous topic of the "death of the author," which during the 1960s and 1970s was elaborated both in literature and in the visual arts, cannot be entirely separated from the absence works we have analyzed. The absence of the artist in that context, given all previous examples (such as the absence of the mimetic approach and the absence of material artworks), appears as the "disappearance of the last criterion of art," to paraphrase Oskar Bätschmann.[42] It can be understood as a disappearance of the very modernist idea that the artist is the last criterion of the modern idea of art. This means that the artist, as a modernist social construct, disappears to make an empty room in which the people can meet and interact. The artist as an "extraordinary individual" vanishes so that creative acts become a property of each human being. Creation in this sense appears out of the unique personal identity that is being constituted in a person's relations with other human beings that can take place in the newly opened absence of the artist. To connect the creation out of nothing with the personal identity is not a contradiction. If we recall the meaning of *nihil* as explained in the beginning, we can find this *nihil* in freedom from the personal identity and personal existence, which is its constitutive feature. In other

---

[42]"Warhol brachte das letzte noch vorhandene Kriterium von Kunst zum Verschwinden, das der Authentizität, die vom Sendungsbewusstsein des Künstlers aufgebaut und von seinem Leben bestätigt wird." Bätschmann, 1997: 215.

words, escaping from one's isolation in order to enter a personal relation is what signifies at the same time the capacity to become a person
and to make a free, creative, and ecstatic movement toward the *other.*

When discussing the issue of the creative act as a means for overcoming individuality, the "absence" works are significant for one more
reason. As we have seen in the analysis of Zizioulas' theology of personhood, the human body, our biological hypostasis, is the clearest
manifestation of individuality. The disappearance of the human body
from the artwork means, in Zizioulas' words, the disappearance of
"the fortress of individualism."[43] In the *Invisible Sculpture* the spectator becomes strongly aware of the body that disappears from the site.
In the case of Rodney's death, the absence makes all those who participate in the project think of the disappearance of the artist's body
as a physical and biological reality. If we understand the human body
in its historical manifestations to be a strong sign of individuality, the
disappearance of the artist's body can be seen as making the space of
creation free from the necessity of the individual presence and not only
from the necessity of pre-given matter. Understanding disappearance
this way does not imply a rejection of the body as evil or unnecessary,
in favor of the spirit or some other existence. It could rather be said that
the body disappears as an individual's "fortress of ego" and a means of
separation. This opens room for the possibility of personal presence in
the absence of body. Christians cannot, of course, reject the body as evil
nor can they look at it as the "prison of the spirit" or as an unessential
part of the human being. Human beings do exist as *bodies*; outside of
them, according to the Orthodox Christian tradition, there is not an
abstract "spirit" that is liberated from the body with the destruction of
the latter. If this were the case, the resurrection of Christ and the resurrection of the dead at the end of history would have no meaning. It is
precisely the resurrection that clearly points to the unique existence of

[43]See Zizioulas, 1985: 52.

each human being. The human body participates in the uniqueness of the human person as a reality that is rescued from decay and is being glorified. The faith in the resurrection after death is a conviction that our bodies will be transfigured in the Heavenly Kingdom and liberated from the constraints of this world and its individual character. On the other hand, as we have seen, the human body exists historically as an individual, biological hypostasis that is sentenced to death since its conception. Therefore, one can even speak of the liberating effect of the disappearance of the human body, without rejecting the body as evil or unnecessary.

The solution to this problem, from a eucharistic and ecclesial perspective, can also be found in some sort of "disappearance" of the body. The necessary destruction of the human body as biological hypostasis, which comes to all humans in the fallen state in the form of biological death as the final consequence of individuality, can paradoxically be transformed into an instrument of liberation and affirmation of personhood. This point is developed by Vasilios Gondikakis in his work *Holy Liturgy—Revelation of the New Creature*:

> A Christian is not buried as a dead body, defeated by illness and time. On the contrary, by dying he is offering himself completely to God, as a Liturgical sacrament. Long time ago, before he biologically died, his own will, fear and hate had died. . . . Not only his will, not only his plans and hopes, but now he offers even his own body to God, the body which is now static and dead. He brings to God his body with joy, offering thanks to God. . . . In this liturgical moment there is a descent and an assumption, one funeral and one raising from the grave: it is sown a natural body, it is raised a spiritual body. The death and the funeral are Eucharistic offerings.[44]

[44]Gondikakis, 1998: 97, 98.

This is a good example of how one and the same phenomenon can have two opposite meanings in Christian anthropology and ontology. Death is the result of the separation from God and is considered the "last enemy" (1 Cor 15.26). However, God uses the same means to save human beings, "trampling down death by death,"[45] in Christ's death. Thus, biological death becomes simultaneously a curse for individual bodily existence and a possibility for personal existence, if put in the right perspective. In death we have an opportunity to finally become liberated from our individuality if we freely offer our body as a liturgical sacrifice. Thus we are also called to "trample down death by death."

I think that a similar logic, although not consciously used to correspond to the religious ideas by any means, can be applied to the above examples of the "absence" works. The physical presence of the artist has been withdrawn to open up the possibility of his presence in his physical absence. A communal dimension of this act can be found in the fact that the physical absence of the artist is manifested only in the presence of other human beings. It is these other persons who start to constitute a personal presence of the artist, who is not there himself or who does not exist any more in his biological hypostasis, by relating to him. Absence of an individual body becomes a sign of "opening a being," of its own withdrawal as an individual in order to appear in a relational, inter-personal context.

* * *

To fully understand this phenomenon and to examine it more closely, we have to return to the concept of *ekstasis* as a basic personal capacity. We have already seen that *ekstasis* represents the personal capacity that enables human beings to begin, even here and now, the transformation of their own individuality into a personal way of existence. We have seen that for Zizioulas *ekstasis* primarily means "getting out" of one's

[45]From the troparion of Pascha.

closedness and individuality. *Ekstasis* then primarily signifies a movement toward *the other*. In that sense, love is ecstatic par excellence,
since through it an individual chooses now to base his or her reality as
a concrete person on the existence of the *other*, as opposed to the *self*.[46]
This reflects the relation between human beings and God, who is the
absolute "other" and, at the same time, the one who gives existence to
human beings in the most literal sense. The roots of human existence
are thus to be found in God's love. Human beings can also accept this
existence only ecstatically, only by "getting out" of their individuality.

Drawing conclusions from the void and absence works we can say
that *ekstasis* should be understood as overcoming individual existence,
but this overcoming of the isolation of individuality and pre-given
presence happens through the encounter with emptiness. My claim
is that both the creative impulse in the examples of art works and the
human attempt to become a person face the same emptiness which
enables their freedom. To illustrate this point I shall give an example
of our daily usage of the pronoun "I" that demonstrates the scale of the
individuality-based ontology. Ecstatic movement appears in this light
as fundamental for both a creative effort and for reaching a new free
existence.

In the state of individuality, which predominantly shapes our
experience, the connection between the pronoun signifying a person's
own identity ("I") and the verb signifying existence ("to be") becomes
unconditionally possible in the present tense, in the form the common
phrase "I am." From the perspective of our daily experience, as well as
grammar, this appears to be a complete expression. It means that existence as such is tied to our individuality, our consciousness, perception,
and the understanding of what and who we are. "I" thus interprets the
verb, which signifies existence as such. It seems that there is nothing

---

[46]This is the reason why the famous Sartre's phrase "hell is other (people)"
can, in this context, be re-phrased as other (people) is both (my) hell and (my)
paradise.

more apparent than to claim that the truth expressed by the phrase "I am" is the basic presumption that precedes all other statements. But this is exactly why the phrase is problematic when considered from an ontological perspective. This phrase mirrors an entire ontology based on understanding existence as either originating from a being, or as a property of a being. Based on these premises we can say that someone or something "possesses" life. That someone or something first "is" and then "exists" in a certain way, manifesting his or her own particular life. From a Christian point of view this ontological premise is problematic as "I" becomes a distorted mirror of God and his tautological claim "I am who I am" (Ex 3.13–15).[47] In light of a Christian anthropology, it is precisely here that the logic of primordial sin lies. Human beings want their existence in such a manner that the self ("I") is the origin of individual ("my") existence. However, if any being in the created universe could be self-sufficient, existing independently from God, it would be another god, another absolute being which monopolizes existence. And yet, God's original plan for human beings was for them to be gods in communion with him; however, gods in a qualified and not absolute sense.[48] Then the origin of human sin does not lie in the desire to become gods but in the desire to become *gods independent from God.*

[47]It is important to note here that God's name in the Hebrew original, in the form of the Tetragrammaton, implies first of all the future tense of the expression ("I am Who will be," "I will be Who I will be" or "I will be") and then also the present and the past tense. See Propp, 1999: 181, 204, 205; cf. also LTK (Jahwe, JHWH), Vol. V: 712, 713, (Tetragramm) Vol. IX: 1358.

[48]Norman Russell shows in his study of the concept of "deification" in the patristic literature that in many instances (e.g., in the thought of St Symeon the New Theologian) "becoming gods" has been understood as the original plan for the human beings, expressed correctly by the serpent (in Eden), but wrongly actualized: "Deification is thus the recovery of the original likeness to God. In a passage which alludes to the serpent's promise, 'you will be like God' (Gen. 3. 5), Symeon says that God 'does not envy mortals when they become equal to him by grace . . . but is glad and rejoices when he sees us, who from being human become by grace what he is by nature' (Hymn 44. 384–93)." Russell, 2004: 302.

This ontological impossibility, as already explained, led human beings to a state of virtual existence—a permanent disintegration. Not only did human beings believe that existence was possible without God, but they also believed that an *individual existence* was an option. This is an ontological impossibility since God himself exists as Persons in communion, and yet it has become the cornerstone of human existence.

This perverted ontology had a serious consequence. It resulted in fear of everything that is outside "me," that is not an individualized "I" or concurred by "I." Even thinking of the potential absence of "me" causes fear, because it signifies the boundaries of an individual and the limitations of individuality-based ontology. This is the reason why death becomes the ultimate horror for the individual. The potential absence of "me" exposes the failure not only of a particular being to grasp existence but of the entire ontology on which human existence is grounded. Consequently, this ontology must always end in a complete skepticism that denies any ontological meaning.

Ekstasis in such a situation means that an individual refuses his isolation and the understanding of existence as an individual's own property. Being ecstatic as an individual entails escaping one's individuality, which means that one admits existence is something not limited only to the "I" but that its source can be outside "me." This movement is meaningless from the point of view of an individuality-based ontology. If "I" projects itself outside "I" that means that "I" can only enter its disappearance and death. That means that crossing the borders of an individual being means entering into its absence.

This is precisely the moment in which the whole ontological paradigm changes: "I" enters his or her own absence to become present in his or her absence. This logic appears to be equivalent to the logic we encountered in the analyzed "absence" works. "I" enters his or her own death, as an individual, to be newly born as a person. This is an existential "jump into the abyss," a jump into "nothingness" in order to exchange the security of "this world" for a free existence.[49] *Ekstasis* here is not simply the "opening up" of a being toward the other; it is a possibility of entering one's absence in order to grasp existence on a different ontological basis. This change requires *metanoia*, a fundamental change of one's mind. In order to exist as a person one must be out of one's own individual mind, one must cross the boundaries of the pre-given reality and isolation.[50] In order to live, we must reject the ontology of "this world."[51] Getting out of the atomized self, both in a creative effort to overcome the necessity of this world and in a love relation, an individual enters the space of one's own absence. But this very act confirms a change in the human relation to one's own existence; human beings reject the pre-given state and individuality as an ontology on which the "self" is based. This attempt of the human being *to be where one is not* is transcendental and demonstrates human free and creative capacities par excellence. It confirms the human being as the *image of God*, since in this ecstatic act the human being tries to stretch his or her existence outside the pre-given state.

This ability of *ekstasis* to lead a being outside its boundaries into "nothing" is linked with another constitutive element of the ecstatic movement—the other. *Ekstasis* can never be a movement toward

---

[49]"I" behaves in this case as a fortress, a clearly marked entity protects its own "existence" and security from intruders. "I" can be secured only as a closed system, since any opening of its borders and boundaries (understood in psychological, existential, as well as political terms) is potentially harmful. This logic is so deeply rooted into our experience as natural being, that it can be seen consistently applied on various levels, from that of particular beings to more complex social and political structures.

[50]This is how the quote "we are fools for Christ's" (1 Cor 4.10) by the Apostle Paul can and perhaps should be interpreted.

[51]A part of this ontology is our mind which, in its fallen state, reflects individualized, fragmented existence. This radical change, to which all humans are called, is illustrated by Christ's words in a number of instances in the Gospels (cf. Mt 10.37; Lk 9.62; 1 Jn 2.15).

nothing or toward one's self alone, as it would collapse again into individuality. It is always a movement toward the other, toward something or someone outside one's self. An ecstatic act is then the projecting of the existence of self outside its individual borders in order to meet the other, to communicate with the other and to be confirmed by the other in this existential quest. This way, paradoxically, something or someone outside me becomes the source of my existence, while the self becomes the reason for an individual's own *kenosis*.

If we look upon *ekstasis* this way, it becomes clear that it is not love exclusively that signifies *ekstasis* as "getting out" of one's isolation for a relational existence, although love is the most apparent and most complete expression of *ekstasis*. The same happens in the human attempt to create. Creation out of nothing becomes possible since it originates from this space "outside" the individual's isolation. Crossing the boundaries of the individual's isolation means entering the *nothingness* of the individual's existence. In an attempt to create, one faces absence as a "field" liberated from the terror of individuality and any pre-given existence. In doing this, one also demonstrates freedom even from pre-determination—a human being refuses the "I am" ontology for a relational existence. This is the reason why entering the *emptiness* or *absence* of our individual existence should also be understood as exercising ontological freedom as a basic property of the person. Together with the ontological freedom, a creative attempt represents a quest for a different ontology, which refuses the boundaries of the individual. A creative act thus appears as having an ecclesial character in itself.

This shows that *ekstasis* can be understood as the foundation of both love and creation. Because both are based on the same foundation, they both lead to overcoming individuality and entering a personal way of existence. At this point we can appreciate human creation ontologically, in light of Christian anthropology and ecclesiology. Based on the creative aspects of the ecstatic movement, we can also say that the Church is not only a communion of human beings that choose love to be the foundation of their being; she is also a communion of creative persons, who "invent" themselves through their relation with God and other human beings outside the pre-given necessity of their natural existence.

This means that the origin of a creative act lies in the human potential to overcome the state of necessity and "get out" of one's individuality. Trying to create, human beings demonstrate a very basic capacity of personal existence—the capacity to overcome the pre-given presence and to bring into existence something that has never existed before. Thus, human creation consists primarily in this ecstatic act and not in artworks as objects or things. A creative act of a concrete human being in this way achieves primacy over objects of art as shaped material. In this ecstatic movement individuality, as the isolation of a being (self-sufficiency, self-identification), with the necessity of the pre-given presence is being overcome.

Based oneself on the foregoing discussion, one might conclude that the creative ecstatic act as a demonstration of human freedom is not bounded by a person's individuality, the pre-given facts, or the pre-given matter and objects that surround us. The ecstatic act originates out of the *ecstatic overcoming of an individual. Ekstasis is going out there,* into the absence of an "I," in order to transform it into a personal presence. "Absence" here should not be understood only in spatial terms, just as the presence of the human being cannot completely be reduced to a concrete space. Just as personal presence depends not only on a physical body but also on a person's energies, absence should, in this context, also be understood as absence in spatial terms as well as in the terms of "energies" of a person, that are both space- and time-related. Thus the problem of time rises as another barrier which limits an individual existence, causing human absence in history.

* * *

We are now able to look at emptiness and absence not only as a tragic necessity with which human beings are bounded, but also as the potential for creation out of nothing. Just as biological death can be considered fatal and tragic but also a potential for the transformation of the ontological foundations of our existence, emptiness and absence in a creative act bear a positive meaning. They represent freedom from all necessary and pre-given presences. It is an opportunity given to man. Although individuality is the most remarkable repercussion of the Fall (and is directly related to death) it also appears here, as a possibility given to man to overcome the Fall and its consequences. A human being can triumph over individuality by "getting out" of himself into his own absence. By choosing his or her individual absence, human beings actualize an ontological freedom. This very act of rejection of the individual existence for a personal freedom becomes a creation, with or without a material manifestation.

Understanding the concept of creation and its relation to the concept of individuality, as they are described here, evidences a tremendous change in the meaning of these categories since the eighteenth century. If we keep in mind the explanation of the individual given earlier, it becomes clear that individuality does not imply something positive. Rather, it signifies the failure of the human being to become a person. If we recall now the capacity of creation as a singularly human capacity, it becomes clear that the capacity of creation does not belong to individuality. This is quite the opposite conclusion compared to the usual understanding of these concepts. We have become so familiar with typically modernist concepts such as the artist, individual, and subject, that we must make an effort to understand the seemingly paradoxical outcome of the former analysis: the concepts of person and individual can be considered as mutually opposite. The same is valid for the concepts of art, as a modern institution, and creation, as a universal human capacity with an ontological significance. Contrary to what might be expected, individuality itself leads to the human inability to create. This causes another situation—since the eighteenth century we have become familiar with the concept of "extraordinary individuals" who are different because they can produce "masterpieces" because of their talent ("genius"). However, just as art can be understood as primarily a bourgeois and a market construct, the idea of "genius" appears as equally ideological and problematic from the point of view of Christian anthropology. Instead of a small number of extraordinary individuals capable of creating art, we have come to the point where creativity belongs to each human being as a part of his/her *image of God*. Thus, the concept of creation becomes alienated from modernist constructs of art and individuality, and instead is used to understand the very existence of the human being. It signifies the uniqueness and extraordinary character of each human being, which is to be actualized in a creative attempt *toward others*.

In the preceding chapters discussion focused on two basic necessities confronting human beings: the pre-given presences in the world, including the compelling presence of human nature, and individuality. The discussion also made it apparent how these necessities can be overcome through a creative act. In the next chapter I address another necessity that can be considered as a special case of the first one: the necessity of time in which human beings historically exist. Time also appears as an instance of emptiness and absence that challenges human existence in the most profound way.

My analysis of the origin of the creative act showed that the human being is confronted with two absences when trying to "get out" of his or her isolation. It is the absence that human beings encounter at the edge of their biological and individual existence. However, human existence is also intrinsically connected to time. Therefore, absence appears as a time category as well; it occurs in the past, when one was not, in the future, when one will be not, but also in the present, having in mind the ongoing disintegration of human beings in the fallen state.

To analyze the meaning of a creative act in relation to the problem of time, I will first present several essential points that characterize a Christian perspective of time.

2.4 Creation and Time

Time belongs to the created world.[52] This understanding of time as a part of the created reality (which is neither "older" nor "younger" than the created world) seems to be established very early in the patristic literature.[53] If time is a created entity that means that it also suffers from the Fall and its consequences. It is maybe the easiest way to demonstrate the state of the fallen world by pointing to the permanent fragmentation and disappearance that characterize our perception of time.[54] Nikolai

[52]Each analysis of time risks creating confusion over the exact meaning of the term, especially if time is analyzed in a biblical perspective. The modern meaning of the word significantly differs from the concept of time we find in the Scriptures, where its primary meaning (among many others) is the "right time for" something (*kairos*). It is strongly connected with concrete events, especially those that mark the flow of the sacred history leading it to the final event—establishing the Kingdom of God (cf. DB: 1001). We also find a tension between the ancient Greek and Roman idea of a cyclical time and the idea of linear time, characteristic of Jewish as well as for Christian understanding of time (although it seems that both of these ideas are indeed present to some extent in ancient Israel, see ABD, Vol. 2: 595).

[53]Panayiotis Tzamalikos holds that Origen was the first one to develop the Christian approach to time (Tzamalikos, 2006: 179). In Tzamalikos's view, Origen's influence might have served as an inspiration for Augustine's philosophy of time (Tzamalikos, 1991; also: Tzamalikos, 2007). (Cf. Augustine's explicit references to time as a creature: Augustinus, *De Gen. ad Litt. Imp. Lib.*, Cap. III, 8.17; *Confession. Orthodox* P. I quest. XXXIII in *Libri Symbolici Ecclesiae Orientalis* (Ernst Julius Kimmel).

[54]It was Augustine who offered the classical description of time in respect to its permanent fragmentation and disappearance: "for the past, is not now; and the future, is not yet" (Augustinus, *Confessiones*, Lib. XI, Cap. XIV, 17), while presence

Berdyaev aptly uses the concept of "evil time" to describe the historical time in which we live, which suffers from the Fall.[55] "Evil time" is time that has been broken into past, present, and future, which represents the disintegration of the world; it is itself individualized, fragmented, and death-bearing.[56]

If we employ time in understanding human creation, we will see that in a creative act the human being tries to overcome not only "here"

is an endlessly small particle of time permanently disappearing between the past and the future.

[55]"Time of our worldly reality, the time of our worldly eon is fragmented time; it is evil time since it contains evilness in itself, the death-bearing principle; it is not an integral time, but fragmented into past, present and future" (Berdyaev, 2001: 79).

[56]Instead of treating time as a separate phenomenon which "flows" (or in which we move) Alan Torrance offers a very important insight into Christian understanding of time according to which we should look at time as one aspect of the spatio-temporal reality (see "Creation ex Nihilo and Spatio-Temporal Dimensions, with special reference to Jürgen Moltmann and D. C. Williams," Torrance, 2004). He criticizes the idea of time as a "passage" (based on the "myth of passage" critique by D. C. Williams and J. J. C. Smart), as this idea of time, in his view, shapes Moltmann's theology of creation when it comes to the temporal issues. Instead of understanding the assumption that we move through time or that time itself moves, Torrance repeats Williams's idea of the world's "manifold occurrences." This means that "we are simply temporally extended beings with thoughts and feelings all of which occupy different spatio-temporal places" (Torrance, 2004: 95). The purpose of Torrance's argument is to explain that the divine act of creation should not be considered as "either located in time or extended in time" (Torrance, 2004: 98) and, consequently, that Moltmann's argument in respect to *creatio originalis* and *creatio continua* is seriously confused. Although this intervention by Torrance might seem self-evident, I find it important to bring this argument into discussion again, since understanding the world as determined in a space-time perspective (rather than understanding the world as being determined, which then *moves* in time toward its end) can shed different light on the topic of the "end of time." Christian eschatology must then be concerned not only with the end of the "time-flow" but also with the *end* (or transformation?) of the entire space-time structure which was brought into existence and which was, as one and the same structure, turned into the fallen state.

as a pre-given reality of one's finiteness, but also "now" as a disappearing fragment of time in which one paradoxically exists. In this way the human being tries to stretch his or her presence over the space-time structure and to express his or her personal existence outside disintegrating time. In such a situation the future seems to be a symbol for overcoming the space-time structure and disintegrating time, since only the future can give a meaning to the present and to the past. In this orientation toward *what is going to be*, one can find an appreciation of the continuum of space-time in its fallen state. *Ekstasis* as projecting one's presence over one's former absence—to "be" where one "is not," requires time. One could even say that what "I am" is not what "I" *actually* am now, but what "I am" spans from the past, through the present, to the end of time. Only the existence that encompasses not only what the human being *is* but what the human being *can* and *will be* can be properly called an integral existence.

This projection of human presence into the future is visible in any movement we make "in order to." It is a demonstration of our faith in future into which our presence is being projected. However, what we expect from the future is not to be simply another disappearing particle of time that will also try to find its meaning in the future coming after it. We actually expect the future to give an ontological validation of the "now." We hope that the future will somehow be integrative, an integral "now" embracing both the present and the past. This perception of time and our own presence in it can clearly be seen in our wish to make a record of each significant event in our private and public life; we hope that the documents (e.g., photographs, audio-video materials) will be there to "prove" our presence in the future time. This "proof" is expected to overcome the boundaries of our physical presence. They will witness to our "now" in the future even after our biological death. The same intention is also manifested in the idea of the continuance of human works, of which the artworks of the past are perhaps the best example. Taking the form of architecture, sculpture, or painting, human works have been produced throughout history to last as long as possible, giving a testimony to the past presences.

Thus, human beings manifest themselves primarily as beings of the future that exist precisely in the possibility of transcending the pregiveness of the "evil time" and all of historical existence, including their own pre-given nature. This way one very paradoxical intention—to stretch one's presence over necessity and time, despite the fact that the only certain perspective of each human being is his or her disintegration and ultimate destruction—becomes a profound feature of what the human being is. In this intention we find the origin of both faith and hope for which no reason or proof can be found within the natural order of things. At the same time, this transcendental aspect of the human being is the origin of our fear of death. Death is the ultimate threat to human presence. It leads to the final necessity manifested in the human inability to express him or herself, inability to communicate and to manifest his or her existence as communion.

From the perspective of time, human creativity appears as a demonstration of the basic human desire to be present in a complete way, transcending the here and now. Projecting one's presence from the present time into the future, creation becomes a quest for overcoming the fragmented evil time and death itself. Creative works seem to be able to carry some of the personal energies of their authors from the present moment into the future, despite the fact that the authors will not biologically exist when their personal energies reach other persons in the future.

Besides this general idea that can be adduced from the artworks, there is also a more specific reference to the problem of time in twentieth-century art. In contrast to previous works, the flow of time in modern and postmodern art often becomes an integral part of a work, not only a frame in which a work appears. This can be seen in the

examples discussed earlier. When, for instance, the visitors-collabora-
tors are moving, talking, or thinking in an empty gallery, they do not
"observe" a complete work (since it is *nothing*) but rather create it all
the time. The work is not completed at one point of time; it is rather
a process, an event being constituted together with the human beings
present, their activities, thoughts, and communications. Time becomes
a constitutive aspect of the creative process and is incorporated into it.
Using time this way is even more visible in the case of Donald Rodney's
project where creation can potentially continue infinitely, depending
exclusively on the persons involved in the process of "communication."

However, despite the fact that time appears as an essential aspect
of human creation in general (with or without artifacts) and that a
creative act discloses the human quest for overcoming the limitations
of the present, neither of these actually solves the problem of a person's
absence in time. If human creation is understood merely as stretching
the presence of one's personal energies over an extended period of time,
then creation will continue to exist in the future particles of fragmented
time, still bounded by the historical time that triumphs over the personal presence. In that sense there is no essential difference between a
creative act whose traces disappear now or in a thousand years. Human
attempts to create, as attempts to overcome one's isolation in order to
stretch one's presence over one's former absence, are then sentenced
to failure. This is true not only in terms of the necessity of pre-given
presence or our individual existence, but also in terms of escaping the
slavery of the fragmented time in which the creative attempt appears.
It seems that the only way to affirm existence as such is to overcome
the fragmented evil time, which itself is caught in its *bad endlessness*.
The problem is that time itself progresses toward its end, which it can
never reach alone, as a realization of its immanent purpose. Its fallen
nature manifests itself in reaching the future that will instantaneously
become the past. The nature of time in its fallen state becomes poten-

tially an *endless* disintegration. In other words, living a permanent disintegration in our time, we live our hell as distance from God and the fulfillment of what man desired in the beginning—existence apart from God. What makes this time different from hell, as an eternal existential solution, is the presence of *hope*—hope that there is a possibility of ending the bad endlessness and that human beings can be liberated from the state of death. Therefore, overcoming the present moment or some future moments can be a psychological consolation to human beings, a satisfaction that someone's works will live longer than the concrete person. However, all attempts to fight against disintegration by securing a longer existence for the traces of our personal presence merely show our fear that transcendence of our individuality in a creative act will end in nothingness and necessity again, confirming our individuality and incapacity to escape the state of death.[57]

[57]Martin Heidegger's brilliant solution to the problem of time, its disintegration, death, and at the same time, existence and truth, can be related to the attempts to make time-ness (*Zeitlichkeit*), and the decay it brings, an immanent part of the very existence of the work of art. Instead of trying to triumph over time by resisting it (as in the famous saying that "everything fears time, time fears the pyramids"), which turns out to be in the long-term an impossible attempt. Heidegger suggests that the meaning of works of art is to reveal the process of disintegration to which all human creation as well as human existence are subjected (cf. Heidegger, 1967: 235–267; and Gianni Vattimo's analysis of Heidegger's famous example of the Greek temple in Vattimo, 1991: 77. Cf. also Kockelmans, 1985: 141–144, 149–167; and Krell, 1986: 155–176). This solution is attractive for many reasons. First of all, it points to the integrity of existence to which I referred earlier. That means that I am not only the one who is "now" but also the one who was the one who will be. What is not yet already belongs to me and to my own identity. The continuity of existence is thus revealed in decay. However, this solution is problematic from a Christian point of view since the state of the world in history (time) is not regular and cannot be taken as the criterion. It is rather a paradox which is to be solved in the process of history and in its climax, the eschaton. The integrity of existence thus makes sense only if it overcomes death, which means only if it is open toward an existence that does not manifest itself as decay and death.

We come to the point when the meaning of time in a Christian view cannot be understood apart from eschatology. Our time will end in a new reality. Therefore, understanding the relation between time and eschatology is a necessary pre-condition for our understanding of the relation between time and human creation.

2.5 Creation, Time, and Eschatology

The meaning of history is, for Christians, revealed in its end, toward which the historical process strives. The "last things" bring "this world" to its end, opening the era of the Kingdom of God. The *eschaton* has often been perceived not only as the "end times" but also as "the end of time."[58] According to this interpretation, history itself brings us to the future point that will be the end of history as well as the end of time; time will cease to exist, becoming the timeless reality (eternity).[59]

[58]See NDT: 329. Justin Popović speaks of the "end times" in his monumental work *Dogmatics of the Orthodox Church*. He states that in the Day of Judgment "time will cease to exist" (Popović, 1978: 747) and continues: "in some mysterious way time will be immersed into eternity" (Popović, ibid.). This interpretation of the eschatological reality, which brings time to an end, is developed on the basis of Rev 10.6. The verse is read literally: "time shall be no more" (Popović, ibid.). However, the sentence from Rev 10.6 cannot be read apart from the next verse (Rev 10.7) where the same sentence continues. When reading these two verses together "the end of time" appears in a different light, as "there would (should) be no more delay, but . . . " or, as Martin Rist and Lynn H. Hough put in *The Interpreters' Bible*, "no time is left for anything that belongs to the old epoch" (IB: 441). This expresses the expectation of the early Church in the immediate parousia and end of history, but cannot be taken as an account that gives any evidence as to the disappearance of time as such. Cf. also Ford, 1975: 160.

[59]The time-eternity dualism, which is frequently present in Christian eschatological discourse, is also problematic, since the content of these words is not clear. Saying simply that time will become eternity in the end (as J. Popović seems to do) does not give any clarification as to the nature of this "eternity." Is it the same timeless reality in which God exists or is this "eternity" in some respects different? The basis for this dualism seems to be very difficult to find in the Scriptures. Cf. also DB: 1001.

But the relation between time and eschatology seems to be more complex than that. If time is a part of the created world it, too, awaits redemption and salvation together with all created beings. Therefore it cannot simply be annihilated in the end as a phenomenon with no ontological meaning. On the other hand, the "end times" bring "this world" to its end, together with the present space-time structure. Christianity, of course, does not radically negate the world but at the same time it does affirm its end and the beginning of a new world, of the "new heaven and new earth."[60] This paradox can be solved through the concept of *transfiguration* which the creature is subjected to. The world will not be destroyed, but rather renewed, established in its true state for the first time. If this general idea is applied to time, we can speak of a different, *eschatological* time, which will not become the timeless reality that we apply to God's existence, neither will it continue to be the fragmented time we experience in history.

As I mentioned earlier, some elements of this understanding of time and its end we find in Berdyaev's philosophy. In his view evil time is a synonym for the disintegration and death we experience in history. However, this time can be overcome through creativity. It is a creative act that is the result of *communion between time and eternity*.[61] Through creativity, eternity conquers evil time. Creativity, therefore, has a liberating effect, bringing the "tyranny of time" to an end. However this timelessness that follows the end of time in the *eschaton* is, in fact, the *true time*.[62] The *eschaton* is the "eternal present," which means it is both temporal and eternal at the same time.[63]

[60]Cf. Is 65.17; Rev 21.1.

[61]See Slaatte, 1988: 35–36.

[62]See Slaatte, 1988: 116.

[63]"Thus, the Apocalyptic end to which Berdyaev refers is the *eschaton*, i.e., the end related to the eternal present, which makes it both temporal and eternal. The *finis* of time is brought about, while its true *telos* is in eternity. Thus we must say, 'The end is the triumph of meaning.'" Slaatte, 1988: 116.

These subtle differences between "evil" time and "true" time, which is also different from the timelessness that we apply to God, have their pre-history in Christian thought. David Bradshaw convincingly shows that already in early patristic literature we can notice three different modes of existence in respect to time.[64] It is, first of all, "diastemic" existence, which has "extension" and "intervals" (Athanasius, Gregory of Nyssa) that characterizes creatures. In contrast to this, "adiastemic" existence, with no "extension, span or measure" characterizes the existence of God.[65] However, in order to explain the eternity of such creatures as angels, it was necessary to differentiate between time and the eternity of God, so we come to another "eternity" that is somehow related to our time. Gregory Nazianzen speaks of the eternity of the angels as a "certain timelike movement and extension."[66] We find a similar usage in Basil's writings where eternity, referring specifically to the original state of creatures, is a movement that "revolves upon itself," ending nowhere.[67] Therefore, the "one day" (not "first") mentioned in Gen 1.5 is actually an image of eternity.[68] This seems to be a pattern which will later be developed. I will mention here only one more instance, John of Scythopolis and his understanding of time, which is in its structure similar in many respects to that of Berdyaev. For John of Scythopolis "eternity" is not only the property of God but also of creatures through their participation in it.[69] In eternity created time ends, existing no more for itself but becoming restored to its original state.

From all these examples one can easily see that "time" is understood as a manifestation of an incomplete existence, something that has to

---

[64]Bradshaw, 2006-a; 2006-b.

[65]Bradshaw, 2006-a: 334–336; 2006-b: 3.

[66]Bradshaw, 2006-a: 338.

[67]Bradshaw, 2006-a: 337.

[68]Bradshaw, 2006-a: 337.

[69]Bradshaw, 2006-a: 343–346. For Maximus the Confessor's understanding of time and eternity see Balthasar, 1961: 136, and further.

be brought to its end, while "eternity" is a concept used with much less clarity, both in respect to God and created beings. We see, however, that there has been a sense of distinction between the time we know in history, "timelike" reality that characterizes angels, and the concept of eternity that is related to the existence of God but can also embrace the existence of created beings.

If we try to understand time-eschatology relations based on these insights, we can conclude that eschatology brings an end to fragmented time since it brings an end to the entire world of necessity. Since evil time is one aspect of the created and fallen world, it finds its meaning in its end, in the eschatological event. It becomes an "eternal present," which means that it becomes the "eighth day" of creation, of which the "one day" is an icon. However, this "eighth day" which refers to the free existence of human beings, together with the rest of created beings, is not a static, motionless reality. It will be an ever growing presence, an everlasting movement in the perfection of love, without any loss. This constant movement brings human beings closer to God, making their existence more and more godlike, but without achieving total identification with God. This clearly implies that this "integral" and "real" time will still be different from the timelessness of God. Eschatological time will be an endless approaching the eternal existence of God.

The relation between time and the *eschaton* requires another clarification before the significance of the human creation in respect to time and eschatology becomes apparent. It is the relation of time to eschatology that takes place already in the course of history.

One feature of time as a part of created reality is that it has no immanent (natural) potential for redemption from the state of disintegration and necessity, which the whole creation awaits. There is no "natural" way for causing the end of "this world." Therefore an intervention from the "outside" was necessary to bring an end to the immanent disintegration of time in history, in order to heal it. This is the reason why the

incarnation of Christ marks the beginning of the end times, the beginning of the end of this world. His incarnation brings the *eschaton* to the
space-time, putting an end to its *evil* endlessness.

From the time of Christ's incarnation, death, and resurrection, history develops toward its end in constant tension between "already" and
"not yet." The Kingdom of God is already granted, but it is still to come.
The *eschaton* is already visibly present in the liturgy, as an icon of the
Kingdom of God. This eschatological reality appears in the Church in
a number of instances: a natural timeline is broken, so the past, present and future appear instantaneously. Christians thus keep a *memory*
of the past and *anticipate* the coming Kingdom of God. But they also,
paradoxically, *recall* what is going to happen and give *a prophecy* of
things that have happened.[70] The Kingdom of God is, therefore, not
simply a future moment that will last forever, nor is it a negation of
God's creation in any of its manifold aspects. The Kingdom of God
comes to us out of the *eschaton*, which means out of the end of this
time, outside the space-time structure of our reality.

---

[70]From this perspective the usage of the verb "to be," which I have discussed
earlier, appears in a different light. The expression, which signifies our existence,
can only be formulated in the future tense, if expressing a Christian ontological perspective. If we refuse individuality as a satisfactory model to describe the existence
of the human being in favor of personhood, we are also forced to reject a definition
of the human being based on the properties which a particular individual possesses. It is not possible then to identify the existence of the indivisible properties
of man (the very *in-dividuality*) with a certain timeframe of our historical existence.
Since a person cannot be reduced to the individual properties of the human being,
the person must be understood as a relational reality. The relational reality of personhood includes the capacity of transcending the temporal boundaries as well as
the physical boundaries of the body or physical surroundings in which the human
being finds him/herself. Paradoxically, the person is not the reality that one can
point a finger to and grasp it in its fullness. In order to grasp one's true identity, "I"
must escape its isolation by performing an ecstatic act. Thus ecstatic acts possess
a temporal dimension that leads the human being, in their final consequence, to
overcome history and escape Berdyaev's "evil time."

These features of time and the *eschaton* allow us to think of another meaning of the tension between "already" and "not yet." Eschatological reality is not entirely absent from time even now, although it will never be entirely present within fallen, evil time. Eschatology, therefore, should not be understood as an event that is a part of fragmented time, but rather as its transformation from deterministic and disintegrating nature into the possibility of "growing" freely. The *eschaton*, in other words, would represent the end of the space-time structure of "this world" as we know it in its compelling and fallen form. It seems to me that the central aspect of this tension is to be found in the very character of the coming Kingdom of God since we do not enter this new reality without our free participation in it. This is the reason why the *eschaton* is already present here as a possibility of participating in it in order to liberate ourselves from the determinisms of this world. Time, and the world in its totality, is already redeemed, but now human beings together with the rest of the created world, have to redeem themselves. This redemption means the acceptance of the Kingdom of God which, and this is the point I want to stress, takes place via a creative act. This is also the reason why salvation cannot be comprehended only as something that lies in the future and has no direct relation with the world as it is. Salvation as changing the mode of our existence begins already "here" and "now,"[71] with human movement toward the Kingdom of God, which is not temporal although it appears in time. In this paradox lies the explanation of how Christians can reject "this world," which "lies in the power of the evil one" (1 Jn 5.19) and, at the same time, appreciate it since it was originally made "good" (Gen 1.4–31). It is "this world," with all its weakness and imperfections, where salvation begins.

These aspects of the Christian understanding of eschatology and the Kingdom of God have direct and profound consequences for our

---

[71]Cf. "This is the day that the Lord has made; let us rejoice and be glad in it." Ps 118.24.

understanding of human creativity and its significance. If we look at the problem of time as described earlier, especially in its relation to eschatology, we can differentiate between two uncertain realities that the human being faces in history. On the one hand, this world in all its dimensions (space-time, energies . . .) has no existence without a relation to God. In that sense creatures are not "real" by themselves nor can their existence be considered *true*. On the other hand, from the perspective of this world's fragmented time, the Kingdom of God is "not yet," so it cannot yet be grasped as a tangible reality, as an objective fact. Its "already" presence can be grasped only through faith. This means that if we take one of these realities as the criterion of truth, they become mutually exclusive. If our present reality is *the* reality, then the *eschaton* is not yet, and vice-versa.

If we return to the question of what kind of absence human beings face when trying to create in terms of time, we are forced to situate this question within the paradox I have just described. The Christian answer to the question of truth and reality is, of course, that they can only be fully grasped in the *eschaton*.[72] However, this eschatological truth and the reality of the Kingdom of God do not have a compelling character. The *eschaton* is the "kingdom of freedom," and freedom is our "ticket" to enter it. Affirmation of our freedom in the *eschaton* is possible precisely because this Kingdom is still "not yet," not "real" from a deterministic perspective. To recognize the *eschaton* as the reality on which one can ground his or her existence requires a creative act that has a liberating effect—it makes human beings free from the world as a state of necessity, enabling them to *see* what still cannot yet be seen.[73] One can observe

[72]In words of St Maximus the Confessor "the old (Old Testament) is a shadow, the new (New Testament) is the icon, and the truth (reality) is the state of the future age." St Maximus the Confessor, *Comments on the Ecclesiastical Hierarchy by Dionysius Areopagite*, PG 4, 137.

[73]Cf. Jn 20.29; Heb 11.1. Cf. also Berdyaev's analyses "Faith and Knowledge" (Berdyaev, 1996-b: 37–75) and "On Christian Freedom" (Berdyaev, 1997: 93–108).

at this point the way in which the concepts of freedom, creativity, and faith are very closely related. Faith appears as a creative movement too, which makes us capable of escaping the state of necessity. It represents the projection of one's existence outside this world and its boundaries. In this sense, faith has a profoundly transcendental character. The origin of faith lies in the human rejection of the present world along with all its compelling aspects. Starting to believe, human beings reject the state of necessity as a satisfactory ontological solution and the foundation of their existence. Instead, believing in an eschatological reality and the "kingdom of freedom," human beings make an *existential turn*—one chooses the uncertainty of freedom to be the foundation of his or her existence. Being still "not yet," the truth of the *eschaton* is not compelling; there is no "evidence" of it except the freedom-bearing faith itself.[74] In order to grasp this future reality and partake in it one must escape his or her isolation through a free and creative act because there is no reality apart from personhood. The ecstatic movement toward personhood as reality is precisely what will be confirmed or rejected in the world to come.

The creative act appears now in a new light. It represents the crossing of the boundaries of individuality in all its dimensions, including the boundaries of one's individual absence in time. The same capacities that were described as essential in this transition from an individual to a person, play the key role in the attempt to overcome the boundaries of one's absence in time as well. *Ekstasis* is the means by which the human being can bridge the present moment of disintegrating time and the *eschaton*. In an ecstatic act the human being crosses the individual

---

[74]Cf. Heb 11.1. This can well be illustrated by another and somewhat unexpected Paul's sentence in respect to Christ's resurrection. Paul connects the truth of Christ's resurrection with our resurrection which is to appear in the *eschaton*: "if the dead are not raised, then Christ has not been raised." 1 Cor 15.16. This is why Christian truth is in the same time comprehensible only in a free and creative act, while the very truth has a liberating effect (cf. John 8.32).

boundaries in their time dimension. This way one enters the *nothing-ness* of his or her individual presence, which means one's own death as an individual. Crossing the border of individual presence in order to meet the *other*, the human being becomes present in his or her previous absence. The human being departs thus through one death, the death in which the human being historically exists, in order to enter another *death*—one's own absence. This way, one becomes "born again," but not in the evil time anymore but in the *eschaton*, in the communion of Christ's body.[75] Thus the "I" can reach its "self" only if it is placed in the eschatological perspective that the expression "I will be," instead of "I am," symbolizes. This ecstatic projecting of one's free presence over the abyss of time causes one's birth in the *eschaton*. *Ekstasis* causes the "openness of a being" toward the eschatological reality. Through this openness the *eschaton* enters history. This ecstatic movement becomes the foundation of creativity, while the origin of human creation in history lies in the *eschaton*.

Since it is "not yet" and not a compelling fact, it represents the state of freedom, emptied of all the necessities of "this world." As a *positive* "nothingness," when viewed from the historical perspective, the *eschaton* enables human creation *out of nothing*. If we recall what has been said earlier about human expanded presence in the act of *ekstasis*, we will understand how the same principle functions when applied to the time-eschaton categories. In an ecstatic act, which is a fundamental aspect of creation, the human being transcends not only his

[75]In his book *The Mystery of Christ*, John Behr points to a very significant moment which is very often overlooked in Christian eschatology. There is an intrinsic connection between salvation and the original creation, as well as our death and our entrance into the new eschatological reality: "Viewed in the light of Christ, beginning with the Savior, creation and salvation are not two distinct actions, but the continual process of God's activity in his handiwork . . . . This process . . . includes human apostasy, the acquisition of the knowledge of good and evil, the experience of sin and death." Behr, 2006: 86.

or her individuality but becomes born again in the *eschaton*. Human presence therefore, becomes expanded; not only in spatial terms or in terms of interpersonal relations, but also in terms of time. One crosses the boundaries of his or her absence in time, becoming present in the *eschaton*. Creation can then be described as a *crack* in time, which enables eschatology to appear in history. Focusing on the eschatological perspective we can say that a creative act can avoid the necessity of pre-giveness, and can appear out of one's absence, turning this absence into a personal presence.

If we look at the relation between creation, time, and the *eschaton* from this perspective we come to another point: the ecstatic entering into one's own absence in time appears as a creation *ex nihilo*. This *nihil* is to be found in freedom as an eschatological reality, which is relieved of any pre-given or compelling facts including one's own compelling presence.

If the creative act is approached this way, it appears as another icon of eschatology in history and as a bridge that makes eschatology already apparent in our historical existence. A creative act then is not only an ecstatic and liberating act which signifies the "opening" of a being toward the other. It becomes also a prophetic act, as it demonstrates freedom from "this world."[76] Creation becomes a prophecy and the prophetic activity also becomes a creative one, as they both make eschatological reality already present, making us free within the boundaries of history. One could say that the logic of the Church and liturgy applies to human creation as well.

If creation is considered a *crack* in time that enables the *eschaton* to appear in disintegrating time, does it mean that human creation can then be related to ecclesiology and soteriology in a more concrete sense? This question almost necessarily arises, given the ecclesiological solution to the problem of individuality discussed earlier. To speak of

---

[76]Cf. Berdyaev, 1996-a, Vol. I: 133–150.

human creativity as an eschatologically significant concept seems to challenge our understanding of liturgy and Church as the very essential *means* of salvation. If one claims the soteriological significance of human creative acts, does that mean that baptism and the Eucharist are not the only way human beings can enter the Kingdom of God, being "born again" in the *eschaton*, through the liturgy as the icon of the Heavenly Kingdom?

The foregoing discussion suggests that creation, just as freedom and love, has both an eschatological and ecclesial character. It has also been explained that a creative act implies communion-communication with other persons. Otherwise, an ecstatic act leads to egoism and individuality. A closer look at ecclesiology shows that the problem here lies in the different levels on which creation and baptism and Eucharist happen. Both require a change in human existence and both are intrinsically linked with freedom, which itself bears an eschatological character. One should therefore also look at baptism as a creative act, which liberates a person from the boundaries of the fallen world. However, we cannot unconditionally accept the opposite statement, namely that each creation also means participation in the liturgy. The situation in this respect is similar to the relationship between creation and love. Although love is both the "ticket" that enables human beings to enter the Kingdom of God and the "greatest" among all things left to human beings (cf. 1 Cor 13.13), bringing ontological liberation from individuality, it alone is not an act of baptism or Eucharist. It witnesses, just as creation witnesses, to the existence of the human being, but it does not necessarily mean that one accepts God's love and communion with him. In spite of the fact that love, in any form it might take, represents the quest for eternal existence by being an icon of the Church via the communion of two or more people, in individual cases it can also mean rejection of the communion with God. A love relation alone cannot guarantee eternal life in the Kingdom of God without a free relation to

God and other beings established through love and faith.[77] The same reasoning can be applied to human creativity. Each creation is an ontological movement, a prophecy about the change of one's existence. It is an expression of the human existential quest—*to be able to be*. However, if it is not related to God, through communion, it misses its point and becomes an impossible project.

From this analysis we can conclude that human creation primarily means liberation from the necessities of this world, which has an ontological character. Human beings cannot simply escape from time as they cannot be miraculously liberated from their created nature. What they *can* do is begin to overcome the boundaries of their created and fallen nature, together with the boundaries of the fragmented time.

Grounding one's creation on nothing or absence in the form of the *eschaton*, the human being becomes free not only from the compelling presence of the world, but also from the necessity of his or her own presence. Creating out of one's absence, the human being becomes present in the *eschaton* in a more realistic way than in history. One's creation, being eschatological in character, can occur "here" and "now" in certain forms (artifacts or ideas for instance) that are iconic in their character. This iconic character manifests itself in its relation to personhood as an eschatological reality. Therefore, human creative works do not have any ontological meaning if they are separated from an eschatological perspective. At the same time, however, human creation, in each possible form it might take, becomes intelligible only through personhood as its target. If we employ aesthetic terminology, we can say that personhood is the ultimate human creation, the greatest "work of art" to which a human being strives.

---

[77]It could also be argued that love which refuses a relationship with God betrays its own ends, bringing it into a paradoxical situation where it can never reach its own immanent purpose.

2.6 "New Creation"

Although primarily connected to the New Testament and Christian eschatology, the idea of "new creation" can already be found in the Old Testament. This idea is strongly connected to messianic expectations. The Old Testament faith expressed hope for a Messiah (*Mashiah, Christos*) sent from God to "deliver Israel from foreign bondage, restore the glories of a former golden age, and inaugurate the ingathering of Israel and God's kingdom of righteousness and peace."[78] It is no surprise, then, that in the Old Testament the topic of the new creation is primarily connected with prophetic literature.[79]

New creation as a means of redemption is also the main motif in the Christian era, but it acquires additional meanings as well. New creation now primarily means redemption from death. There is, however, another radically "new" moment that occurs in the history of the "New Israel"—the appearance of Christ. Christ appears not as a political leader, or a mere prophet, but a *new being,* the God-man (Θεάνθρωπος). In this sense, with Christ human beings and creatures are granted more blessings than they received in the original paradise. We could also say that Christ's incarnation would have happened even without the original sin, since it was the only way to show the mysterious depths of God's love by which all humans are called to become "gods," by his mercy.[80] In Christ is revealed what human nature is. Being human means the potential to overcome what the human being *is* and to reach what the human being has the potential to become. Thus

[78]ODJR: 458.

[79]The concept of "new creation" can be found in the Psalms but it is primarily the topic of prophesies by Isaiah, Jeremiah and Ezekiel. Cf. Ps 51.10; Ps. 104.29–30; Is 42.9, 18, 19; Is 43.19; Is 49.3–6; Jer 31.31–34; Ezek 11.19–20; Ezek 36.26, 27.

[80]Cf. Athanasius of Alexandria: "He, indeed, assumed humanity that we might become god." *De Incarnatione* 54:3, PG 25, 192 B. Cf. also St Symeon the New Theologian: "Why did God become man? . . . So that man might become god." Symeon the New Theologian (*Eth.* 5. 31–4), quoted in Russell, 2004: 301.

divinity, granted by the mercy of God, becomes the target of human existence, and this godlike existence is what God prepared for "those who love him" (1 Cor 2.9). This will be completed in the Kingdom of God, but it already began with Christ's incarnation. In Christ's person we find the "new creation" in which both the uncreated divinity and the created humanity exist together, within the one single person of the God-man. In this new reality, as "the only thing really new under the sun,"[81] are revealed all the dimensions I have pointed to earlier: (1) ecclesial—since Christ is the Church, being not only the Head of the Church as his body, but existing also as a communion of the divine and human nature; (2) soteriological—since he is the Savior who redeems the human being from death, so that all who partake of Christ become "new creatures";[82] (3) eschatological—since he is the Messiah in whom the expectations of the Old Testament are fulfilled, opening the new *eschatological* times, in which we expect his return and his eternal Kingdom already granted to mankind.

Although the new creation re-establishes communion with God, it is not a simple return to the original state of the world, before the Fall. It is rather a new communion, the Church, as an image of the Kingdom to come. The new creation is then primarily the reality of the Church. This reality is composed of the newly born persons in whom the "old man" died and the "new man" is born.[83] In this sense we could also say that each person is a "new creation," born "from above." However, establishing the Church is only the beginning of the new creation[84] where we will be able to see the reality "face to face" (1 Cor 13.12). In a difference from the original creation, when God was the only Creator who called everything into existence, in the new creation human beings also

[81] St John the Damascene, *The Orthodox Faith*, III, 1, PG 94, 984.

[82] "Therefore if any man be in Christ, he is a new creature" 2 Cor 5.17. Cf. also Gal 6.15 and Rev 21.5.

[83] Cf. Rom 6.1–11.

[84] 1 Cor 15.52; cf. 1 Cor 15.22–54.

participate. The creators of this new eschatological reality are both God and human beings, since man was made in the beginning as an "open project," a being that has to grow in order to grasp his existence with his freedom and in communion with God. Human existence should be affirmed as ontologically free existence, which means that this task would lie in front of the human being even without original sin and the Fall. This is what God could not do for man, something that requires human initiative and creative effort.

This new reality of the new heaven and new earth "no eye has seen, nor ear heard, nor the human heart conceived." (1 Cor 2.9). The most important subject of the new creation is the new persons, human beings liberated from death, individuality, and slavery of every sort. They will be free even from their created nature, becoming truly similar to God. In a difference from history, their existence will be the result of their freedom; they will exist because they freely accepted their existence in communion with God. This creative movement leads into the "outside," in the "nothingness" of human absence that one enters as a personal, relational being. The aim of a creative act is to reach personal existence.

New creation reveals the final meaning of each particular human creation. Its target is the person itself, a new identity and new life that transcends the boundaries of created nature and individuality. It is the world in which human beings will be deified (*theosis*), existing, following St Gregory Palamas, not only *with no end* but also *with no beginning* (origin).[85] This means that no essence or being should be a necessity; no essence as pre-existing reality will exist apart from persons. A being is constituted in an ecstatic act rather than in any substance or individual quality. This is how Christian Triadology influences Christian

[85]"If grace were not unoriginate, how would one become through participation in this grace 'unoriginate like Melchisedec, of whom it is said that his days had no beginning and his life no end'?" St Gregory Palamas, *Triads*, New York: Paulist Press, 1983: 106.

anthropology in a very basic way and the way we perceive human creativity. The act of overcoming our individuality is the act of transforming our being into a *living* relational existence. Through this we achieve an existence which, by the mercy of God, becomes *God-like* instead of *world-like*. This ecstatic act of overcoming the fact of existence for an act of communion requires a creative task. It is laying the foundation of our existence not on anything created, but on the abyss of freedom and love. These capacities transcend every substance and become the material out of which human beings can create their own existence. We become able to "invent" ourselves, but only in relationship to God. If contemplated from this perspective, creativity becomes a basic anthropological concept. In this way human creative capacities are transferred from an aesthetic to an ontological category.

CHAPTER 3

Conclusions and
Perspectives

At the very beginning of this work I pointed to the intrinsic connection between the capacity of creation and freedom. If human beings are to be considered ontologically free beings, they must also be considered creative beings. Creative capacities and freedom must be affirmed if Christianity is to have an optimistic anthropology. However, we face the problem of how to connect the idea of ontological freedom and the presence of pre-given reality, given the impossibility of deriving freedom from pre-given necessity. The final liberation and creation *ex nihilo* thus appear as an existential "jump into nothing," since *nothing* as the absence of any necessity or pre-given reality can alone enable ontological freedom. There is a danger that the reality of "this world" could be rejected for some other (e.g., "spiritual") world that makes this freedom possible. Such a position would be, of course, incompatible with the biblical understanding of God's creation as essentially good.

However, we face the problem of how to connect the idea of ontological freedom and presence of the pre-given reality, given the impossibility of deriving freedom from pre-given necessities. The final liberation and creation *ex nihilo* appear thus as an existential "jump into nothing," since *nothing* as absence of any necessity and pre-given realities can alone enable the ontological freedom. Here occurs a danger that the reality of "this world" will be rejected for some other (e.g. "spiritual") world which makes this freedom possible. Such a position would be, of course, incompatible with the Biblical understanding of God's creation as essentially "good."

We have seen that this issue can be solved by putting the problem of freedom and creation in the context of our individual existence in history where the presence-in-absence paradox occurs. Artistic practices play an important role, since they help us invert the meaning and potential of the presence-in-absence phenomenon. Creation and freedom appear here as a potential to bring things into a free personal presence, which changes their way of existence. We find their origin in "nothing," the absence of individuality. This absence enables a free creation as a manifestation of personal presence. The result is that absence becomes a way to expand one's personal presence, crossing the boundaries of individuality. To enter this personal presence means to leave the individual ("I"-based) ontology, which manifests itself finally as a "zero-ontology" which cannot secure its existence alone.

If the question of human creation is approached this way, rather than as an aesthetical or artistic phenomenon, one can identify very profound connections between the human capacity of creation and human existence as person. It becomes impossible to think of a genuine creation or personhood without pointing to the transcendental aspect of each of them. Both require the transcendence of one's pre-given being in order to reach the reality of freedom. In other words, the boundaries of my own presence, my own "I", have to be challenged and crossed in a creative act as part of our quest for a personal, free existence. We find the means for this in *ekstasis*, which is a central concept in understanding both the creative capacities of the human being and human existence as person. This concept helps us comprehend the puzzling questions of how a creative act can appear within the world of necessity without rejecting it, and how an individual can move toward personhood.

Ekstasis makes absence not only a special case of experiencing *nothing*, which would be a threat for individual existence, but turns it into an opportunity for human beings. On the one hand, we speak of nothingness as the foundation of our natural existence that manifests itself as nothing outside the relationship with God. On the other hand we are aware of nothingness as absence of any pre-given realities that limit our existence, making possible the affirmation of our freedom. We can speak of "negative" and "positive" meaning of *nothingness* and *absence*. The negative nothingness is encapsulated in the nothingness as a necessity. The positive nothingness is always at stake when we, through *ekstasis*, try to depart the "I"-based ontology in order to ground ourselves on freedom, as a relational existence. This becomes a potential, a chance given to a being to overcome one's present state of necessity and individuality in order to grasp one's true identity in freedom.

Because of this, the question that George Steiner raises in the *Grammars of Creation*: "Why is there not nothing?"[1] instead of "something," can be articulated rather differently. There is, indeed, *nothing* on both ends of the creation. Nothing is the foundation of created beings but, at the same time, human beings also enter nothingness to be "born again" and to acquire a free existence.[2]

The further development of the idea of freedom points out that overcoming the pre-given state of our natural existence and individuality necessarily implies overcoming the entire space-time structure that limits human existence. An existential "jump into nothing," in order to acquire a free existence, also means crossing boundaries of the disintegrating time in which our individual existence is rooted. Therefore the nothing that makes freedom and genuine creation possible appears in the *eschaton*. Only *there* can a free existence and creative act be fully manifested. Leaving the security of the "I"-based ontology and historical existence, one enters the insecurity caused by the absence of

[1]See Steiner, 2001: 32.

[2]A comparison with the baptismal ritual and its symbolism seems appropriate here: one enters the water of baptism (water being a typical biblical symbol of death) to exit the baptismal pool as a newly born being.

pre-given realities. In this insecurity, in which one does not find any determinism or pre-given hold, one's ontological freedom can fully be realized. This movement toward the reality of the *eschaton* makes both genuine freedom and creation really present in history. Therefore through a free and creative event the *eschaton* becomes present even in the disintegrating time. This existential movement changes the mode of existence from the necessity of the pre-given state to the *unoriginated* and *uncreated* existence.

This is the reason why our disappearance from this space-time structure is a manifestation of nothingness, both as a threat and a potential. Entering nothingness as an abyss of freedom, a being is liberated from the constraints of this world that have their roots in nothingness. Thus with one nothingness one is liberated from the original nothing, which represents absolute necessity. By negating the original nothingness one affirms an absolute freedom and a godlike existence.

The same paradox is apparent in human biological death. On the one hand, biological death is a necessity in the fallen world. It is the final consequence of the forces that drive our own nature in its fallen state. Our biological death also becomes an opportunity, a potential to fully manifest our personal existence. Entering *my own* death, not as a necessity but voluntarily, as a liturgical sacrifice which is freely offered to God, has a liberating effect, destroying the fortress of *my* ego, individualism. Experiencing death this way, one finally enters a free relation with God, which becomes a new birth. In this way "the last enemy," which is the absolute necessity, becomes the way to perfect freedom. The final absence of an individual leads to the resurrection of a person.

The result is that freedom can be affirmed despite the presence of all the necessities that limit human existence, such as created nature, the compelling presence of this world and, finally, our individuality. The liberation of our world, which takes place through human creative acts, is liberation from a world of necessity, for the free existence of the entirety of God's creation. Human nature should be considered as being precisely *what it is not (yet)*. It is its very character, to transcend itself and reach what lies outside its boundaries, that belongs to it by the *likeness* of God. In other words, human nature exists as freedom, which is to be affirmed in a personal existence. This makes its existence god-like in a very profound sense. Through this capacity of human beings, who are responsible for the virtual existence of the world in history, the entire creation of God has an opportunity to exist as a part of free personal reality.

This brings us to the conclusion that the origins of human personhood and human creativity are basically identical. Their intrinsic connection can also be seen in the communal dimension of the analyzed examples of modern and contemporary artistic practices. They are manifested in *ekstasis* of the individual "self." Through *ekstasis* an individual overcomes the "I"-based ontology, bringing personal presence into the emptiness of the previous personal absence. *Ekstasis* makes it possible for human creative acts to be manifested as *events*, iconizing communion as the fundamental aspect of personhood. Therefore, both human creation and human person, to paraphrase Elisabeth Groppe, appear "*ex nihilo*" and "*ex amore*."[3]

* * *

In analyzing the example of Yves Klein's "Void," I referred to the concept of *techne* and *techne*-elements as something that has historically been overcome in the artistic creation. This phenomenon allows us to reflect on the history of art and its potential significance for understanding human creativity as a theological category.

Reduction of material and perceptual elements in twentieth-century art, especially in relation to conceptual art, has been famously

[3]See Groppe, 2005.

characterized by Lucy Lippard and John Chandler as the "demateri-alization" of art.[4] Arthur Danto characterized the same reduction of material/perceptual elements in a broader sense as "turning art into philosophy," which itself brings an end to the story of art as we knew it.[5]

With "void" as well as "absence" works, art not only rejects particular material and perceptual elements, but turns to be *nothing* (as art). This tendency within modern and contemporary art should be considered a part of broader tendencies in the history of art. As indicated earlier, this coming to "nothing," to the "zero-ontology" of art in the twentieth century is only the final consequence of a process that began a couple of centuries ago. The beginning of this process can be traced back to the birth of our modern understanding of art, which took place in the eighteenth century. Art became something different from *techne* or *arts* of the previous epochs. While some of the *techne*-based disciplines (painting, sculpture, architecture) were embraced in the new category of "fine arts," their meaning and content changed. From *techne* as a practical knowledge, which can be materialized manually through skill, "art" becomes a concept whose primary aim is a "disinterested aesthetic pleasure." In fact, the idea that the aesthetic (sensuous) pleasure is the primary concern of fine arts was the reason for claiming their distinct quality and autonomy among other disciplines.[6] This, together with other concepts that began to be used as essential properties of fine arts, such as genius, inspiration, creativity or imagination,[7] strength-ened the idea that art is an autonomous discipline which should explore its own means and contents.

Further developments in the history of nineteenth century art clearly show this tendency to "liberate" art from all elements and

[4]Lippard, 1971: 255–276.
[5]Danto, 1984; 1997.
[6]Cf. Shiner, 2001: 67–145.
[7]See Džalto, 2010: 6–7.

purposes that are not inherent to art as art. I have argued elsewhere that this tendency to reduce art to *its own content and means* and to liberate art from all elements that are not exclusively artistic, is a manifestation of the quest for the autonomy of art which led art into a gradual reduction of its elements.[8] This process, which went through various stages, culminates in the reduction not only of all elements that previously characterized art as *techne* (e.g., manual execution of a piece and mimesis), but also the rejection of every form of material manifestation of art. At the end, as we have seen in the examples of Warhol's and Rodney's works, even the artist's presence can be annihilated in the process of creation. This is a sign of a growing tendency that affirms some sort of *ex nihilo* creation over the *techne*-elements and aesthetics as the "true" nature of art.

One way to reflect theologically upon this process is to look at it as a process of liberation of art from the necessity of this world embodied in the *techne* elements mirroring the ancient cosmology. From this perspective one can understand the phenomena of nothingness and absence as the victory of faith in human creativity and human ontological freedom over the determinism of the pre-given state as our final destiny. Thus liberation affirms human creativity as something that transcends the boundaries of the pre-given world as well as the boundaries of a special discipline. Human creation, in fact, starts to affirm human personal presence as the source of creation, not any particular talent or the formal properties of particular works. If looked at this way, the modern idea of art appears as one stage in the affirmation of the human capacity to create and has a universal character that is not limited to any particular form or discipline. That means that the purpose of art as a modern social construct is revealed precisely in its disappearance. Its existence is iconic, its meaning is to give a prophecy and foretaste of creation that is the fundamental property of what being

[8]See Džalto, 2010.

human really means. All other concepts used to characterize it, such as imagination, divine inspiration, and others, serve basically as symbols pointing to the "space" of freedom where the human being can be manifested in his or her real personal identity. From this we can also learn that each person should be considered a free and creative being that cannot be equated with natural, political, social, and economic constraints that limit the existence of each human being. This way, the concept of creation that entered Western civilization from the Judeo-Christian tradition is affirmed by particular developments in modern art from *within*, not because their intention was to imitate religious narratives. Ironically and paradoxically enough, these developments within modern art were envisioned precisely to liberate art from all other ends but exclusively "artistic" ones.

From this point of view, certain tendencies within twentieth-century art can be seen as an attempt to affirm a specific anthropology, related to human creation and creativity, that is comparable to those clearly developed in Christian theology. Moreover, this affirmation, with *absence* and *nothing* as the source of creation, went beyond anything that theology has done before (apart from Christian mysticism and apophaticism). In this sense, the developments within twentieth-century art bear a great potential for contemporary theological anthropology. This compels us to think very differently about creativity as a theological category, compared to the traditional approach of theological aesthetics.

One can also take a rather different approach to the phenomenon of nothingness and absence as the culmination of the modern art developments. If one looks at the context of the eighteenth century, in which the very modern idea of art was born, one will be able to see that the concept of art was born primarily as a social institution of a new bourgeois social class, which was rising at that time. In that sense, "fine" or "polite arts" corresponded to the foundation of the "polite

[9]See Shiner, 2001: 79–98.

classes,"[9] who used art as a means of self-affirmation as well as a power-ful political, ideological, and social tool. This thesis could be supported by a number of examples, starting from the purpose that the modern institutions of art, such as museums, galleries, and art schools, were supposed to fulfill, under the general idea of their autonomy and disin-terest. Maybe the most telling example in this respect is the formation of the Louvre museum. When the monarchy collapsed, paintings, and sculptures were used to promote the revolution and the newly born social and political elite. According to Larry Shiner, this was precisely what initiated the preservation of works of fine art in this period, col-lecting and exhibiting them in the new national museum.[10] This de-functionalization of paintings and sculptures by taking them out of their previous political context (which signified their "old" meaning) and placing them into the "neutral" context of the national museum for the sake of their aesthetical value, was a revisionist political interven-tion par excellence. This influenced the later development of the idea of "art for art's sake." The "purposeless beauty" that people could enjoy while contemplating artworks exhibited in the museum was used to de-politicize those very works and turn them from their previous function and meaning, while at the same time employing them to support the new social and political system that was emerging.[11] Such examples of the very subtle ideological function of "pure art" can be seen in nearly every period following the establishment of the new idea of art. This tendency culminates in *abstract expressionism* as the peak of autono-mous or self-referential art. According to Clement Greenberg, in this type of art the very medium of painting comes to the realization of its autonomy, through some sort of "self-consciousness."[12] However, the same autonomous and self-conscious art (as art) can be read as just

[10]See Shiner, 2001: 180–186.
[11]See Shiner, 2001: ibid.
[12]Cf. Greenberg, 1960.

another means of the political propaganda within the context of the Cold War. Just as *social realism* should have expressed the reality of the "new brave world" of communism, *abstract expressionism* should have witnessed to the "freedom" of the capitalist world, with its supposed plurality, individualism and possibility of self-expression.

Such understanding of art as, above all, a social and ideological institution (with a huge web of particular institutions, such as museums, galleries, art journals, art fairs etc.) sheds a different light on the idea of the autonomy of art. "Autonomous art" appears then primarily as a useful ideological construct which was presented as art's immanent purpose. This "conspiracy of art," to paraphrase Baudrillard, is verified in the end when art, looking for its "real" and autonomous identity, ended in *nothing*. In other words, nothingness manifests itself as the only possible content of autonomous art, since there is no "anything" that constitutes this autonomy apart from its social and ideological function. In this way, nothingness becomes the real nature of the modern idea of art, which is revealed in the moment when art reaches a sort of Hegelian "self-consciousness." One could remark, somewhat cynically, that *die Kunstgeschichte* (art history) became *das Kunstgericht* (the judgment of art).

Through the gradual reduction of all elements that traditionally characterized art, one comes to the conclusion that art as it was envisioned in the early modern times came to a point where it split into different phenomena. This split also bears a theological significance.

In a certain sense, art continues to be what it has been since the formation of the concept in the eighteenth century—it continues its existence as a social and ideological function. It continues to be a very profitable business, which is, whenever necessary, employed in telling ideological and political narratives, occasionally performing even purely propaganda purposes. No particular value, form or content is required to call something art—its *function* as art within the art world and a particular society is what justifies a certain object or phenom-enon as *art*. Art as art (to paraphrase Joseph Kosuth) becomes a more effective political tool than art as obvious propaganda.

On the other hand, we can also speak of art in a broader and more conservative way. This second meaning of art still inherits the *techne*-elements. This art tries to affirm these elements through the concepts of aesthetic pleasure, sensuous experience, beauty, or skill. This under-standing of art, unlike the first one, penetrates into many different human activities and products, giving them more conventional artistic, skilled, or beautiful (sensuous) qualities.

Finally, we can also speak of "creation" as the third product of the split within the modern idea of art. Creation as a particular capacity of human beings becomes divorced from art as a particular discipline. Human creativity which reaches *nothing* can be seen as a quest for the liberation from any necessity that has dominated art as a social institu-tion. This creation out of emptiness affirms the human quest for free-dom in a very profound way. It manifests itself as a universal human capacity, which is related to the personal identity of each human being. It, moreover, challenges art as a system but also all traditional con-cepts such as genius and talent as projections of the social and political power.

* * *

To conclude, the human capacity of creation *ex nihilo* can be under-stood as human creation out of person's presence in absence. Absence and emptiness/nothingness become the "free space" out of which one can create. It represents *nothing* as a human freedom from the pre-existing matter. We have seen, however, that this affirmation of creation as a human personal presence need not necessarily be manifested as a rejection of objects. Objects can, as in Duchamp's case, be brought into a personal presence. Bringing them into a personal presence is an act that changes their existence. They are moved from the necessary presence as pre-given facts into a free personal presence. In this way, creation becomes an *event of personhood*, a witness to the possibility of personal existence, of both human beings and the entire world.

Genuine human creation, then, should not be considered a fiction in a theological reflection on human creativity. Instead, it should be understood as a process, an event that is both historical and eschatological. In an analogy to freedom, which already *is* although its source is found in the *eschaton* ("not yet"), creation in history becomes an icon of the eschatological creation out of nothing, which is yet to be completed. This is the creation of a "new creature" as a personal existence in communion with God.

This is the reason why human creation out of nothing is an expression of human existential freedom, no matter what form it might take. The human person appears as the main "topic," the main "subject," and "object" of each creative attempt. In a way quite similar to God's creation, the human being can and should create at the same time *out of nothing* and *out of love*.

2010

Bibliography

Ades, Dawn, Neil Cox, and David Hopkins, 1999: *Marcel Duchamp*. London, Thames & Hudson.

Anderson, B.W., 1962: "Creation" in: IDB, 725–732.

Andreopoulos, Andreas, 2006: *Art as Theology. From Postmodern to the Medieval*. London, Equinox.

Astley, Jeff, David Brown, and Ann Loades (Eds.), 2003: *Problems in Theology: Creation*. London and New York, T&T Clark.

Badt, Kurt, 1968: *Kunsttheoretische Versuche*. Cologne, M. DuMont Schauberg.

Baker, Kenneth, 1998: *Minimalism*. New York, Abbeville Press.

Balthasar, Hans Urs von, 1961: *Kosmische Liturgie—das Weltbild Maximus' des Bekenners*. Einsiedeln, Johannes Verlag.

Barton, John (Ed.), 2003: *The Cambridge Companion to Biblical Interpretation*. Cambridge, Cambridge University Press.

Bathrellos, Demetrios, 2004: *The Byzantine Christ: Person, Nature, and Will in the Christology of Saint Maximus the Confessor*. New York, Oxford University Press.

Bätschmann, Oscar, 1997: *Ausstellungskünstler, Kult und Karriere im modernen Kunstsystem*. Cologne, DuMont.

Bayer, Oswald, 1999: *Gott als Autor, Zu einer poietologischen Theologie*. Tübingen, Mohr Siebeck.

Begzos, Marios P., 1993: "Nikolaj Berdjaew und die byzantinische Philosophie: zur metaphysischen Tragweite der patristischen Theologie," in: *Theologie* 64, Jan–Feb 1993. Also available at: http://www.myriobiblos.gr/texts/german/begzos.html

Behr, John, 2006: *The Mystery of Christ*. Crestwood, NY, Saint Vladimir's Seminary Press.

Berdyaev, Nikolai, 1944: *Slavery and Freedom*. New York, Charles Scribner's Sons.

Berdyaev, Nikolai, 1965: *Christian Existentialism*. New York, Harper & Row.

Berdyaev, Nikolai (Nikolaj Berđajev), 1996-a: *The Meaning of the Creative Act* (Smisao stvaralastva). Vol. I, II, Belgrade, Logos Ant.

Berdyaev, Nikolai (Nikolaj Berđajev), 1996-b: *Philosophy of Freedom* (Filosofija slobode). Vol. I, Belgrade, Logos Ant.

Berdyaev, Nikolai (Nikolaj Berđajev), 1997: *Philosophy of Freedom* (Filosofija slobode). Vol. II, Belgrade, Logos Ant.

Berdyaev, Nikolai (Nikolai Berđajev), 1998: *Spirit and Freedom* (Duh i sloboda). Belgrade, Logos Ant.

Berdyaev, Nikolai (Nikolaj Berđajev), 2001: *The Meaning of History* (Smisao istorije). Belgrade, Dereta.

Bernstein, J. M., 1992: *The Fate of Art—Aesthetic Alienation from Kant to Derrida and Adorno*. University Park, The Pennsylvania State University Press.

Bourdon, David, 1989: *Warhol*. New York, Harry N. Abrams.

Bouteneff, Peter C., 2008: *Beginnings: Ancient Christian Readings of the Biblical Creation Narratives*. Grand Rapids, MI, Baker Academic.

Braaten, Carl E., and Robert W. Jenson (Eds.), 2002: *The Last Things— Biblical and Theological Perspectives on Eschatology*. Grand Rapids, MI—Cambridge, William B. Eerdmans Publishing Co.

Bradshaw, David, 2006-a: "Time and Eternity in the Greek Fathers," in: *The Thomist*, 70/2006, 311–66.

Bradshaw, David, 2006-b, *Christian Approach to the Philosophy of Time* (conference paper). available at: http://www.uky.edu/~dbradsh/papers/Christian%20Approach%20to%20Phil%20of%20Time.pdf

Bremer, Thomas (Ed.), 2008: *Religion and the Conceptual Boundary in Central and Eastern Europe*. Hampshire and New York, Palgrave MacMillan.

Brown, Frank Burch, 1989: *Religious Aesthetics: A Theological Study of Making and Meaning*. Princeton, NJ, Princeton University Press.

Brown, Frank Burch, 2000: *Good Taste, Bad Taste, and Christian Taste*. Oxford, Oxford University Press.

Buchloh, Benjamin H. D., 2000: *Neo-Avantgarde and Cultural Industry*. Cambridge, MA, The MIT Press.

Burghardt, Walter J., 1957: *The Image of God in Man, According to Cyril of Alexandria*. Woodstock, MD, Woodstock College Press.

Bychkov, Oleg V., James Fodor (Eds.), 2008: *Theological Aesthetics after von Balthasar*. Aldershot and Burlington, Ashgate.

Bychkov, Victor, 1993: *The Aesthetic Face of Being: Art in the Theology of Pavel Florensky*. Crestwood, NY, Saint Vladimir's Seminary Press.

Bychkov, Victor (Viktor Bičkov), 2010: *Aesthetics of the Church Fathers* (Estetika otaca Crkve). Belgrade, Službeni glasnik.

Carroll, Noël, 1999: *Philosophy of Art—A Contemporary Introduction*. London and New York, Routledge.

Carroll, Noël (Ed.), 2000: *Theories of Art Today*. Madison, The University of Wisconsin Press.

Casiday, Augustine, 2009: "Georges Vasilievich Florovsky," in: *The Blackwell Companion to the Theologians* (Edited by Ian S. Markham). Chichester, Blackwell Publishing, 46–65.

Caudwell, Christopher, 1977: *The Concept of Freedom*. London, Lawrence & Wishart.

Chirban, John T., 1996: *Personhood: Orthodox Christianity and the Connection Between Body, Mind and Soul*. Westport, CT, Bergin & Garvey.

Christou, Panayiotis (Hristu Panajotis), 1999: *The Mystery of God. The Mystery of Man* (Tajna Boga. Tajna čoveka). Belgrade, Faculty of Orthodox Theology.

Clarke, Norris W., 1998: *Person and Being*. Milwaukee, WI, Marquette University Press.

Congdon, D. W., 2007: "'A Pre-Appearance of the Truth': Toward a Christological Aesthetics," in: *The Princeton Theological Review*, Vol. XIII, No. 1, Iss. 36, 35–50.

Cottrell, Jack, 1983: *What the Bible Says about God the Creator*. Joplin, MO, College Press.

Danto, Arthur C., 1964: "The Artworld," in: *The Journal of Philosophy* (Edited by John H. Randall), Vol. LXI, 571–584.

Danto, Arthur C., 1984: "After the End of Art," in: *The Death of Art* (Edited by Barel Lang). New York, Haven Publishing, 3–76.

Danto, Arthur C., 1997: *After the End of Art: Contemporary Art and the Pale of History*. Princeton, NJ, Princeton University Press.

Danto, Arthur C., 1998: *The Wake of Art: Criticism, Philosophy and the Ends of Taste*. Amsterdam, Overseas Publishers Association.

Danto, Arthur C., 2009: *Andy Warhol*. New Haven, CT, Yale University Press.

Dickie, George, 1974: *Art and the Aesthetics, an Institutional Analysis*. Ithaca, NY, Cornell University Press.

Didi-Huberman, Georges, 1999: *Was wir sehen blickt uns an: Zur Metapsychologie des Bildes*. Munich, Wilhelm Fink.

Dronov, Michael, 2004: "Die Person und die interpersonale Beziehung in der Theologie der östlichen Kirche des 20. Jahrhunderts. Quellen und Entwicklungstendenzen," in: *Phänomenologie der Religion, Zugänge und Grundfragen* (Edited by Markus Enders and Holger Zaborowski). Freiburg and Munich, Verlag Karl Alber, 353–365.

Duchamp, Marcel, 2008: "The Richard Mutt Case," in: *Art in Theory 1900–2000, An Anthology of Changing Ideas* (Edited by Charles Harrison, Paul Wood). Blackwell Publishing, 252.

Dutton, Denis, and Michael Krausz (Eds.), 1981: *The Concept of Creativity in Science and Art*. The Hague, Boston, and London, Martinus Nijhoff Publishers.

Duve, Thierry de, 1996: *Kant after Duchamp*. Cambridge, MA, The MIT Press.

Džalto, Davor, 2007: *The Role of the Artist in Self-Referent Art*. Berlin, Dissertation.de.

Džalto, Davor, 2010: "Creation vs. Techne: The Inner Conflict of Art" in: *Analecta Husserliana: Art Inspiring Transmutations of Life* (Edited by

Patricia Trutty-Coohill). Vol. 106, London and New York, Springer, 1999, 199–212.

Elkins, James, 2004: *On the Strange Place of Religion in Contemporary Art*. New York and London, Routledge.

Eriksen, Paul Daniel, 1989: *The Concept of Person: Zizioulas, Lossky and Arch. Sophrony*. Saint Vladimir's Orthodox Theological Seminary (Thesis).

Ernst, Joseph, 2009: "Gottebenbildlichkeit" in: LTK, 871–878.

Evdokimov, Paul, 2001: "Culture and Faith" in: *The "Foolish" Love of God* ("Luda" ljubav Božja). Chilandar Monastery, Mount Athos, 67–84.

Evdokimov, Paul, 2004: "Modern Art in the Light of Icon" (Moderna umetnost u svetlu ikone), in: *Orthodoxy and Art* (Pravoslavlje i umetnost). Belgrade, Neanika.

Florensky, Paul (Павел Александрович Флоренский), 1915: *The Meaning of Idealism* (Смысл идеализма). Sergiev Posad.

Florensky, Pavel, 2002: *Beyond Vision: Essays on the Perception of Art*. London, Reaktion Books.

Florovsky, Georges V., 1972: *Bible, Church, Tradition: An Eastern Orthodox View, Collected Works*. Vol. 1, Belmont, MA, Nordland Publishing Co.

Florovsky, Georges V., 1974: *Christianity and Culture, Collected Works*. Vol. 2, Belmont, MA, Nordland Publishing Co.

Florovsky, Georges V., 1976: *Creation and Redemption, Collected Works*. Vol. 3, Belmont, MA, Nordland Publishing Co.

Florovsky, Georges V., 1975: *Aspects of Church History, Collected Works*. Vol. 4, Belmont, MA, Nordland Publishing Co.

Florovsky, Georges V., 1987: *The Eastern Fathers of the Fourth Century, Collected Works*. Vol. 7, Belmont, MA, Nordland Publishing Co.

Ford, Massyngberde J., 1975: *The Anchor Bible—Revelation* (Introduction, Translation and Commentary by J. Massyngberde Ford). Garden City and New York, Doubleday & Company.

Francis, Mark (Ed.), 2004: *Andy Warhol. The Late Work*. Munich, Prestel Verlag. (Exhibition catalogue)

Funke, Anna-Elisabeth, 1995: *Metaphysik der Materie und künstlerische Kreativität.* Dettelbach, Röll.

Ganssle, Gregory E. (Ed.), 2001: *God and Time—Four Views.* Downers Grove, IL, InterVarsity Press.

Ganssle, Gregory E., and D. W. Woodruff (Eds.), *God and Time: Essays on the Divine Nature.* Oxford, Oxford University Press.

Goldie, Peter, and Elisabeth Schellekens (Eds.), 2007: *Philosophy and Conceptual Art.* Oxford, Oxford University Press.

Gondikakis, Vasilije, 1998: *Holy Liturgy—Revelation of the New Creature* (Sveta liturgija—otkrivenje nove tvari). Novi Sad, Beseda.

Greenberg, Clement, 1960: "Modernist Painting," in: *Forum Lectures.* Washington, DC, Voice of America.

Greenberg, Clement, 1999: *Homemade Aesthetics—Observations on Art and Taste.* Oxford and New York, Oxford University Press.

Groppe, Elizabeth, 2005: "Creation Ex Nihilo and Ex Amore: Ontological Freedom in the Theologies of John Zizioulas and Catherine Mowry LaCugna," in: *Modern Theology* 21/3, 463–469, 473–476, 478–484.

Groys, Boris, 2008: *Art Power.* Cambridge, MA, The MIT Press.

Gunton, Colin E. (Ed.), 2004: *The Doctrine of Creation: Essays in Dogmatics, History and Philosophy.* New York, T&T Clark.

Heidegger, Martin, 1967: *Sein und Zeit.* Tübingen, Max Niemeyer Verlag.

Hoeps, Reinhard, 1992: "Theophanie und Schöpfunsgrund. Der Beitrag des Johannes Scotus Eriugena zum Verständnis der *creatio ex nihilo*" in: *Theologie und Philosophie.* Freiburg, Herder, 67. Jahrg. Hft. 2, 161–191.

Hoeps, Reinhard (Ed.), 2005: *Religion aus Malerei? Kunst der Gegenwart als theologische Aufgabe.* Paderborn and Munich, Ferdinand Schöningh.

Hopkins, David, 2000: *After Modern Art 1945–2000.* Oxford and New York, Oxford University Press.

Hopko, Thomas, 1963: *The Notion of Hypostasis in Orthodox Theology.* Saint Vladimir's Orthodox Theological Seminary (Thesis).

Hubbard, Moyer V., 2004: *New Creation in Paul's Letters and Thought.* Cambridge, Cambridge University Press.

Jenson, Robert W., 2004: "Aspects of a Doctrine of Creation" in: *The Doctrine of Creation: Essays in Dogmatics, History and Philosophy* (Edited by Colin E. Gunton). London and New York, T&T Clark, 17–28.

Judovitz, Dalia, 1995: *Unpacking Duchamp: Art in Transit*. Berkley, University of California Press.

Kant, Immanuel, 1977: *Kritik der Urteilskraft*. Vol. X, Frankfurt am Main, Suhrkamp.

Kimmel, Ernst Julius, 1843: *Libri Symbolici Ecclesiae Orientalis*. Jenae: Apud Carolum Hochhausenium.

Knight, Douglas H. (Ed.), 2007: *The Theology of John Zizioulas: Personhood and the Church*. Hampshire and Burlington, Ashgate.

Kockelmans, Joseph J., 1985: *Heidegger on Art and Art Works*. Dordrecht, Martinus Nijhoff Publishers.

Koestler, Arthur, 1964: *The Act of Creation*. London, Hutchinson & Co.

Kooten van, George H. (Ed.), 2005: *The Creation of Heaven and Earth, Reinterpretations of Genesis 1 in the Context of Judaism, Ancient Philosophy, Christianity, and Modern Physics*. Leiden and Boston, Brill.

Kosuth, Joseph, 1991: *Art After Philosophy and After: Collected Writings*. Cambridge, MA, MIT Press.

Krahmer, Catherine, 1974: *Der Fall Yves Klein, Zur Krise der Kunst*. Munich, R. Piper & Co. Verlag.

Krell, David Farrell, 1986: *Intimations of Mortality: Time, Truth, and Finitude in Heidegger's Thinking of Being*. University Park and London, The Pennsylvania State University Press.

Krieger, Verena, 2007: *Was ist ein Künstler?* Cologne, Deubner Verlag.

Kris, Ernst, and Otto Kurz, 1980: *Die Legende vom Künstler—ein Geschichtlicher Versuch*. Frankfurt am Main, Suhrkamp.

Kubat, Rodoljub, 2007: "יהוה—The Making-Himself-Present-God of the Old Testament" (יהוה– oprisutnjavani Bog Starog Zaveta), in: *Bogoslovlje*, LXVI, 1–2, Belgrade, Faculty of Orthodox Theology, 93–104.

Kuspit, Donald, 2004: *The End of Art*. Cambridge, Cambridge University Press.

Liddell, Henry George, and Robert Scott, 1996: *A Greek-English Lexicon*. Oxford, Clarendon Press.

Lippard, Lucy R., 1971: *Changing: Essays in Art Criticism*. New York: Dutton, 255–76. (Original version: Lucy Lippard, John Chandler: "The Dematerialization of Art" in: *Art International* 12/2, February 1968, 31–36).

Lossky, Vladimir, 1976: *The Mystical Theology of the Eastern Church*. Crestwood, NY, Saint Vladimir's Seminary Press.

Lossky, Vladimir, 1985: *In the Image and Likeness of God*. Crestwood, NY, Saint Vladimir's Seminary Press.

Louth, Andrew, 2002: *St. John Damascene: Tradition and Originality in Byzantine Theology*. Oxford, Oxford University Press.

Lubardić, Bogdan, 2003: *Between Ungrund and the Father* (Između Ungrunda i Oca). Belgrade, Brimo.

Macherey, Pierre, 1978: *A Theory of Literary Production*. London, Routledge & Kegan Paul.

Macherey, Pierre, 1995: "Creation and Production," in: *Authorship: From Plato to the Postmodern* (Edited by Seán Burke). Edinburgh, Edinburgh University Press.

Mansfield, Elizabeth (Ed.), 2002: *Art History and Its Institutions—Foundations of a Discipline*. London and New York, Routledge.

Mantzaridis, Georgios, 2003: *Time and Man* (Vreme i čovek). Belgrade, Faculty of Orthodox Theology. I.

Marion, Jean-Luc, 1991: *God Without Being*. Chicago, The University of Chicago Press.

Markham, Ian S. (Ed.), 2009: *The Blackwell Companion to the Theologians*. Chichester, Blackwell Publishing.

May, Gerhard, 1978: *Schöpfung aus dem Nichts—die Entstehung der Lehre von der creatio ex nihilo*. Berlin, Walter de Gruyter.

McLeod, Frederic G., 1999: *The Image of God in the Antiochene Tradition*. Washington, DC, The Catholic University of America Press.

Melissaris, Athanasios, 1997: *Orthodox Anthropology and Archetypal Psychology: Comparing John Zizioulas and James Hillman on Personhood.* Boston University (Dissertation), 27–57, 88–107.

Meyendorff, John, 1983: "Creation in the History of Orthodox Theology," in: *Saint Vladimir's Theological Quarterly,* Vol. 27/1, 1983, 27–37.

Milbank, John, Catherine Pickstock, and Graham Ward (Eds.), 2002: *Radical Orthodoxy—A New Theology.* London and New York, Routledge.

Moffitt, John F., 2003: *Alchemist of the Avant-Garde: The Case of Marcel Duchamp.* Albany, State University of New York Press.

Moltmann, Jürgen, 1997: *God in Creation: An Ecological Doctrine of Creation.* London, SCM Press.

Moore, Edward, 2004: *Origen of Alexandria and St. Maximus the Confessor: An Analysis and Critical Evaluation of Their Eschatological Doctrines.* Saint Elias School of Orthodox Theology (Dissertation).

Nahm, Milton C., 1965: *Genius and Creativity: An Essay in the History of Ideas.* New York, Harper Torchbooks.

Newman, Michael, and Jon Bird (Eds.), 1999: *Rewriting Conceptual Art.* London, Reaktion Books.

Northcott, Michael S., 2005: "Concept Art, Clones, and Co-Creators: The Theology of Making," in: *Modern Theology* 21/2, 219–236.

Ottmann, Klaus (translation, introduction), 2007: *Overcoming the Problematics of Art—The Writings of Yves Klein.* Putnam, CT, Spring Publications.

Papanikolaou, Aristotle, 2004: "Is John Zizioulas an Existentialist in Disguise? Response to Lucian Turcescu" in: *Modern Theology,* Vol. 20/4, October 2004, 601–607.

Papanikolaou, Aristotle, 2006: *Being with God: Trinity, Apophaticism, and Divine-Human Communion.* Notre Dame, IN, University of Notre Dame Press.

Pattison, George, and D. O. Thompson (Eds.), 2001: *Dostoevsky and the Christian Tradition.* Cambridge, Cambridge University Press.

Pattison, George, 2005: *Thinking about God in an Age of Technology.* Oxford, Oxford University Press.

Pattison, George, 2008: "Is the Time Right for a Theological Aesthetics?" in: *Theological Aesthetics after von Balthasar* (Edited by Oleg V. Bychkov and James Fodor). Aldershot and Burlington, Ashgate, 107–114.

Perović, David, 2007: "The Concept of God's Name in the Holy Scriptures and by the Church Fathers" (Pojam Imena Božijeg u Svetom Pismu i kod crkvenih otaca), in: *Istina*, 19–21/2007, 45–55.

Peters, Tiemo Rainer, and Claus Urban (Eds.), 1989: *The End of Time? The Provocation of Talking about God*. Mahwah, NJ, Paulist Press.

Plevnik, Joseph, 1989: *What Are They Saying about Paul and the End Time?* Mahwah, NJ, Paulist Press.

Pontzen, Alexandra, 2000: *Künstler ohne Werk: Modelle negativer Produktionsästhetik in der Künstlerliteratur von Wackenroder bis Heiner Müller*. Berlin, Erich Schmidt.

Pope, Robe, 2005: *Creativity: Theory, History, Practice*. New York, Routledge.

Popović, Justin, 1978: *Dogmatics of the Orthodox Church* (Dogmatika pravoslavne crkve). Vol. 3, Belgrade, Ćelije Monastery.

Porteous, N. W., 1962: "Image of God" in: IDB, Vol. 2, 682–685.

Prettejohn, Elizabeth, 2005: *Beauty and Art 1750–2000*. Oxford and New York, Oxford University Press.

Propp, William H. C., 1999: *The Anchor Bible—Exodus 1–18*. New York and London, Doubleday.

Quasten, Johannes, 1986: *Patrology*. Westminster, MD, Christian Classics.

Restany, Pierre, 2005: *Yves Klein: Fire at the Heart of the Void*. Putnam, CT, Spring Publications.

Richards, Ruth (Ed.), 2007: *Everyday Creativity and New Views of Human Nature: Psychological, Social, and Spiritual Perspectives*. Washington, DC, American Psychological Association.

Richardson, Cyril C. (Ed.), 2006: *Early Christian Fathers*. Louisville, KY, Westminster John Knox Press.

Rickards, Tudor, Mark A. Runco, and Susan Mogeret (Eds.), 2009: *The Routledge Companion to Creativity*, London and New York, Routledge.

Robinson, Dominic, 2011: *Understanding the "Imago Dei"—The Thought of Barth, von Balthasar and Moltmann*. Burlington, VT, Ashgate.

Rosenstein, Leon, 2002: "The End of Art Theory," in: *Humanitas*, Vol. XV, No. 1, 32–58.

Russell, Norman, 2004: *The Doctrine of Deification in the Greek Patristic Tradition*. Oxford and New York, Oxford University Press.

Sartre, Jean-Paul, 1993: *Being and Nothingness*. New York, Washington Square Press.

Sauve, Ross Joseph, 2010: *Georges V. Florovsky and Vladimir N. Lossky: An Exploration, Comparison and Demonstration of Their Unique Approaches to the Neopatristic Synthesis*. Durham University (Doctoral Thesis), available at: *http://etheses.dur.as.uk/591*

Sawyer, Keith R., 2006: *Explaining Creativity: The Science of Human Innovation*. Oxford and New York, Oxford University Press.

Schwarz, Arturo, 1969: *The Complete Works of Marcel Duchamp*. New York, Harry N. Abrams.

Schweppenhäuser, Gerhard, 2007: *Ästhetik—Philosophische Grundlagen und Schlüsselbegriffe*. Frankfurt am Main, Campus Verlag.

Seigel, Jerrold, 1997: *The Private Worlds of Marcel Duchamp: Desire, Liberation, and the Self in Modern Culture*. Berkeley and Oxford, University of California Press.

Shevzov, Vera, 2004: *Russian Orthodoxy on the Eve of Revolution*. Oxford, Oxford University Press.

Shiner, Larry, 2001: *The Invention of Art: A Cultural History*. Chicago, University of Chicago Press.

Skira, Zenon Jery, 1998: *Christ, the Spirit and the Church in Modern Orthodox Theology: A Comparison of Georges Florovsky, Vladimir Lossky and John Zizioulas*. Toronto School of Theology (Dissertation).

Skliris, Stamatis, 2005: *Through a Glass, Darkly* (U ogledalu i zagonetki). Belgrade, Faculty of Orthodox Theology.

Slaatte, Howard A., 1988: *Time, Existence and Destiny—Nicholas Berdyaev's Philosophy of Time*. New York, Peter Lang.

Sophocles, E. A., 1914: *Greek Lexicon of the Roman and Byzantine Periods (From B.C. 146 to A.D. 1100).* Cambridge, MA, Harvard University Press.

Speiser, A. E., 1964: *The Anchor Bible—Genesis* (Introduction, Translation and Notes by E. A. Speiser). Garden City, NY, Doubleday & Company.

Stallabrass, Julian, 2004: *Art Incorporated: The Story of Contemporary Art.* Oxford and New York, Oxford University Press.

Steiner, George, 1989: *Real Presences.* Chicago, The University of Chicago Press.

Steiner, George, 2001: *Grammars of Creation.* New Haven, CT, Yale University Press.

Stuhlman, Byron David, 1991: *An Architecture of Time: A Critical Study of Alexander Schmemann's Liturgical Theology.* Duke University (Dissertation).

The Princeton Theological Review, 2007: Vol. XIII, No. 1/36 (Theology and the Arts), Spring 2007, Princeton, NJ, Princeton Theological Seminary.

Thompson, John, 1994: *Modern Trinitarian Perspectives.* New York and Oxford, Oxford University Press, 83–85, 124.

Thunberg, Lars, 1995: *Microcosm and Mediator—The Theological Anthropology of Maximus the Confessor.* Chicago, Open Court.

Tibbs, Eve M., 2006: *East Meets West—Trinity, Truth and Communion in John Zizioulas and Colin Gunton.* Fuller Theological Seminary Pasadena (Dissertation), 16–18, 34–42, 65–118.

Torrance, Alan J., 1996: *Persons in Communion.* Edinburgh, T&T Clark.

Torrance, Alan J., 2004: "*Creatio ex Nihilo* and the Spatio-Temporal Dimensions, with special reference to Jürgen Moltmann and D. C. Williams" in: *The Doctrine of Creation: Essays in Dogmatics, History and Philosophy* (Edited by Colin E. Gunton). London and New York, T&T Clark, 83–103.

Turcescu, Lucian, 2002: "'Person' versus 'Individual,' and Other Modern Misreadings of Gregory of Nyssa," in: *Modern Theology* 18/4, 527–539.

Turner, Denys, 1999: *The Darkness of God—Negativity in Christian Mysticism.* Cambridge, Cambridge University Press.

Tzamalikos, Panayiotis, 1991: "Origen and the Stoic View of Time," in: *Journal of the History of Ideas*, Vol. 52, No. 4, Baltimore, The Johns Hopkins University Press, 535–561.

Tzamalikos, Panayiotis, 2006: *Origen: Cosmology and Ontology of Time.* Leiden and Boston, Brill.

Tzamalikos, Panayiotis, 2007: *Origen: Philosophy of History & Eschatology.* Leiden and Boston, Brill.

Vanhoozer, Kevin J. (Ed.), 2003: *The Cambridge Companion to Postmodern Theology.* Cambridge, Cambridge University Press.

Vattimo, Gianni, 1991: *The End of Modernity* (Kraj moderne). Novi Sad, Bratstvo-Jedinstvo.

Vogel, Arthur Anton, 1963: *The Christian Person.* New York, Seabury Press.

Volf, Miroslav, 1998: *After Our Likeness: The Church as the Image of the Trinity.* Grand Rapids, MI, William B. Eerdmans.

Wallis, Brian (Ed.), 1999: *Art After Modernism: Rethinking Representation.* New York and Boston, The New Museum of Contemporary Art, David R. Godine.

Ward, Graham (Ed.), 2005: *The Blackwell Companion to Postmodern Theology.* Malden and Oxford, Blackwell Publishing.

Westermann, Claus, 1976: *Genesis.* Neukirchen-Vluyn, Neukirchener Verlag.

Wooden, Anastacia, 2010: "Eucharistic Ecclesiology of Nicolas Afanasiev and Its Ecumenical Significance: A New Perspective," in: *Journal of Ecumenical Studies*, 45/4, 543–560.

Yannaras, Christos (Janaras Hristo), 2005: *Metaphysics of Body* (Metafizika tela). Novi Sad, Beseda.

Yannaras, Christos, 2007: *Person and Eros*. Brookline, MA, Holy Cross Orthodox Press.

Zangwill, Nick, 2007: *Aesthetic Creation*. Oxford and New York, Oxford University Press.

Zizioulas, John, 1969: "Some Reflections on Baptism, Confirmation and Eucharist," in: *Sobornost*, 5, 9/1969, 644–652.

Zizioulas, John, 1970: "God Reconciles and Makes Free—An Orthodox Comment," in: *Bulletin of the Department of Theology of the World Alliance of Reformed Churches and the World Presbyterian Alliance*, Vol. X, 2/1970, 7–8.

Zizioulas, John, 1975: "Human Capacity and Incapacity," in: *Scottish Journal of Theology* 28, 401–448.

Zizioulas, John, 1985: *Being as Communion: Studies in Personhood and the Church*. Crestwood, NY, Saint Vladimir's Seminary Press.

Zizioulas, John, 1992: "On Being a Person. Towards an Ontology of Personhood," in: *Persons, Divine and Human. King's College Essays in Theological Anthropology* (Edited by Christoph Schwöbel and Colin E. Gunton). Edinburgh, T&T Clark, 33–46.

Zizioulas, John, 1994: "Community and Otherness," in: *Saint Vladimir's Theological Quarterly* 38, 347–361.

Zizioulas, John, 1997: "Identity of Modern Man" (Identitet savremenog čoveka), in: *Iskon* 4, 18–20.

Zizioulas, John, 2001: *Eucharist, Bishop, Church: The Unity of the Church in the Divine Eucharist and the Bishop During the First Three Centuries*. Brookline, MA, Holy Cross.

Zizioulas, John, 2006: *Communion & Otherness: Further Studies in Personhood and the Church*. London, T&T Clark.

Zizioulas, John, 2008: *Hellenism and Christianity* (Jelinizam i hrišćanstvo—susret dva sveta). Belgrade, Christian Cultural Center.

Zizioulas, John, 2009: *Lectures in Christian Dogmatics*. London, T&T Clark.

Zizioulas, John, 2009: *Remembering the Future: An Eschatological Ontology*. London, T&T Clark.

Zizioulas, John, 2010: *The One and the Many*. Alhambra, CA, Sebastian Press.

Lexicons, Dictionaries and Encyclopedias

AB: *The Anchor Bible—Genesis,* 1964: Introduction, Translation and Notes by E. A. Speiser, New York, Doubleday.

ABD: *The Anchor Bible Dictionary*, 1992: Edited by David Noel Freedman, Vol. 2, 5, New York, Doubleday.

DB: *Dictionary of the Bible*, 1963: Edited by James Hastings, New York, Charles Scribner's Sons.

DTIB: *Dictionary for Theological Interpretation of the Bible*, 2005: Edited by Kevin J. Vanhoozer, London, Baker Book Co.

EDR: *Encyclopedic Dictionary of Religion*, 1979: Edited by Paul Kevin Meagher, Thomas C. O'Brien and Consuelo Maria Aherne, Washington, DC, Corpus Publications.

EP: *Enzyklopädie Philosophie*, 2010: Edited by Hans Jörg Sandkühler, Hamburg, Felix Meiner Verlag.

HWP: *Historisches Wörterbuch der Philosophie*, 1974: Edited by Joachim Ritter, Vol. 3, Darmstadt, Wissenschaftliche Buchgesellschaft.

HWP: *Historisches Wörterbuch der Philosophie,* 1989: Edited by Joachim Ritter and Karlfried Gründer, Vol. 7, Darmstadt, Wissenschaftliche Buchgesellschaft.

IB: *The Interpreter's Bible,* 1957: Edited by George Arthur Buttrick (Comentary Editor), Vol. 12, New York and Nashville, TN, Abingdon Press.

IDB: *The Interpreter's Dictionary of the Bible*, 1962: New York and Nashville, TN, Abingdon Press.

LTK: *Lexikon für Theologie und Kirche*, 2009: Edited by Walter Kasper, Vol. I–XI, Freiburg, Herder.

DT: *The New Dictionary of Theology*, 1989: Edited by Joseph A. Komonchak, Mary Collins and Dermot A. Lane, Wilmington, DE, Michael Glazier.

NHTG: *Neues Handbuch teologischer Grundbegriffe*, 1984: Edited by Peter Eicher, Vol. 1–4, Munich, Kösel.

ODJR: *The Oxford Dictionary of the Jewish Religion*, 1997: Edited by R. J. Zwi Werblowsky and Geoffrey Wigoder, New York and Oxford, Oxford University Press.

PGL: *A Patristic Greek Lexicon*, 1961: Edited by G. W. H. Lampe, Oxford, Clarendon Press.

Illustrations

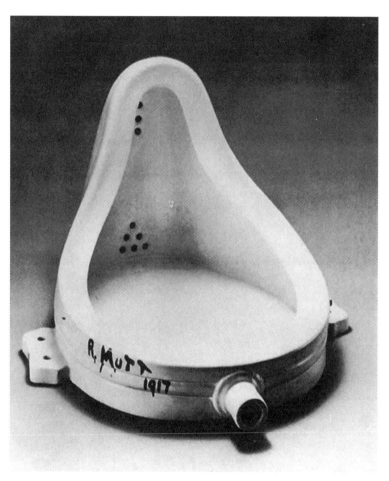

1. Marcel Duchamp, *Fountain*, 1917

2. Yves Klein, *Le Vide*, 1958

3. Richard Long, *A Line Made by Walking*, 1967

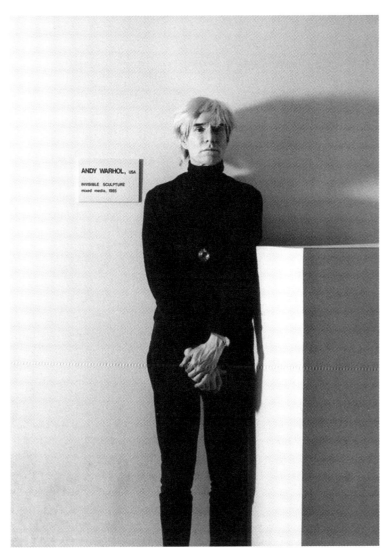

4. Andy Warhol, *Invisible Sculpture*, 1985

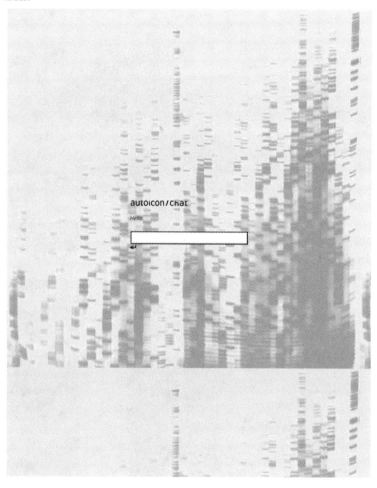

5. Donald Rodney, *Autoicon*, initiated in 1998.
(Webpage Print)